Favourite Family Games

Favourite Family Games

CHOSEN BY CELEBRITIES

Introduced by
John Alderton and
Pauline Collins

MICHAEL JOSEPH
LONDON

MICHAEL JOSEPH LTD

Published by the Penguin Group
27 Wrights Lane, London W8 5TZ
Viking Penguin Inc., 375 Hudson Street, New York, New York
10014, USA
Penguin Books Australia Ltd, Ringwood, Victoria, Australia
Penguin Books Canada Ltd, 10 Alcorn Avenue, Toronto, Ontario,
Canada M4V 3B2
Penguin Books (NZ) Ltd, 182-190 Wairau Road,
Auckland 10, New Zealand

Penguin Books Ltd, Registered Offices: Harmondsworth,
Middlesex, England

First published in Great Britain 1993

Typeset in Goudy 10/13 point
Printed and bound in Great Britain by
Butler & Tanner Ltd, Frome and London
Design and computer page make-up by Penny Mills

A CIP catalogue record for this book is available from the
British Library

ISBN 0 7181 3693 4

The moral right of the author has been asserted

All royalties from this book are to be donated to:

LEUKAEMIA
RESEARCH FUND

43 Great Ormond Street, London WC1N 3JJ
Telephone: 017-405 0101

CONTENTS

Publisher's note   15
Introduction   17

PENCIL AND PAPER GAMES

Consequences   23
THE EARL OF BRADFORD

The Poetry Game   24
NICHOLAS MOSLEY
Variation: 25
THE MARQUESS OF ANGLESEY

Limerick Game   25
LEUKAEMIA RESEARCH FUND

Add Your Own Line to a Famous Poem's First   26
LEUKAEMIA RESEARCH FUND

Scrub a Fairy   27
ROSIE THOMAS

A European Game   28
CHRISTOPHER MARTIN-JENKINS

Literary Styles   28
THE RT HON VIRGINIA BOTTOMLEY MP

The Dictionary Game   29
RUMER GODDEN
Variation: 30
IAN AND KATHY BOTHAM

The Quotation Game   31
SIR IAN McKELLEN
Variation: 31
SAM LLEWELLYN

The Dictionary Game – with Books   32
DIANA RIGG

5

Variations: 32
CHRISTOPHER MARTIN-JENKINS
SIR JEREMY MORSE
HELEN ATKINSON WOOD
CHERYL CAMPBELL
NATASHA RICHARDSON
SANDI TOKSVIG

Advertising 34
DAMON HILL

Headlines 35
THE RT HON NORMAN LAMONT MP

Blind Man's Dip *or* The Game 36
EMMA NICHOLSON MP

Boy Girl Boy Girl *or* The Alphabet 37
Game *or* Categories
JIMMY MULVILLE
Variation: 38
ROSEMARY CONLEY

The Drawing Game or Pictionary 38
LORD OAKSEY
Variation: 39
SIMON WILLIAMS

Battleships 39
GORDON HONEYCOMBE

OUTDOOR AND TRAVELLING GAMES

Kick the Can 45
IMOGEN STUBBS
Variation: 45
LUCINDA GREEN

Balloon Treasure Hunt 46
WENDY CRAIG

CONTENTS

Biblical Treasure Hunt   47
RABBI LIONEL BLUE

The Bellman   47
JOHN TOVEY

A Beach Game   48
CLAIRE RAYNER

Guess the Profession   48
NICK AND GILL FALDO

Arms and Legs   49
LESLIE CROWTHER

Cricket on the Move   50
RACHEL HEYHOE FLINT

Dog Spotting   50
ROBERT ROBINSON

The Car Numbers Game   51
CLIFF MICHELMORE AND JEAN METCALFE

Number Plates   51
CLAIRE RAYNER

A Stay-awake Game   53
SAM LLEWELLYN

THESPIAN GAMES

Charades   57
HIS ROYAL HIGHNESS THE DUKE OF KENT

Adverbs *or* In the Manner of the Word   58
THE COUNTESS OF LONGFORD
Variation: 58
MICHAEL BUERK

Silent Chinese Whispers   59
MICHAEL YORK

Rhyming Dumbshow   59
JANE ASHER

The Game   60
JANET SUZMAN
Variation: 62
JEREMY BEADLE

The Return of the Emperor   63
BERYL BAINBRIDGE

I Went to Paris   65
WILLIE CARSON

WORD GAMES

What Am I?   69
IAN MESSITER

Twenty Questions *or* Who Am I?   70
TONY JACKLIN
Variations: 71
FRED SECOMBE
JANE SEYMOUR
SARAH GREENE

The Hat Game   71
NIGELLA LAWSON

If You Were ...   73
NANETTE NEWMAN

Botticelli   74
SAM LLEWELLYN

The Railway Carriage Game   76
GYLES BRANDRETH MP

Proverbs   76
RICHARD BRANSON

Wrong Name Game   77
MIN HOGG

Taboo   78
THE EARL OF YARMOUTH

CONTENTS

Monosyllables 78
THE RT HON LORD WILSON OF RIEVAULX

Crambo 79
IAN MESSITER

Numerical Phrases 80
HONOR BLACKMAN

The Tennis-Elbow-Foot Game 80
MICHAEL ASPEL
Variation: 81
CLIFF MICHELMORE AND JEAN METCALFE

Poet's Chair 81
Variations: 82
THE RT HON SIR DAVID STEEL MP

Wanderer's Game 83
IAN MESSITER

I Love My Love 83
PAMELA ARMSTRONG

Prime Rhymes *or* Stinky Pinky 85
SUE COOK

How, When, Where and Why? 86
JAMES HUNT

Ghost 87
JEREMY PAXMAN
Variation: 87
IAN MESSITER

Gritty Uvula 88
DAME JUDI DENCH

Description Switch 89
MIN HOGG

Frances Hodgson Burnett's Game 90
GYLES BRANDRETH MP

AFTER-DINNER GAMES

Up Jenkins   95
THE RIGHT REVD RICHARD HARRIS, BISHOP OF OXFORD

Fizz-Buzz   96
DR PATRICK MOORE

Clapping Games   96
ANNEKA RICE

The Animal Game   97
LEUKAEMIA RESEARCH FUND

Category One Two   98
MIKE GATTING

Ping-Pong Table Football   99
BOB WILSON

Murder by Winking   100
DAVID JACOBS

Scissors, Paper and Stone   101
JULIAN PETTIFER

A Dice Game   101
PAUL DANIELS

Chinese Whispers   102
LINDA BELLINGHAM

CARD GAMES

Spoons   107
FELICITY KENDAL

Pairs   108
COLIN COWDREY

Shop Snap   108
MAUREEN LIPMAN
Variation: 109
LEUKAEMIA RESEARCH FUND

CONTENTS

Cheat   109
GARETH HUNT

Old Maid   110
RORY UNDERWOOD

Caboosh   111
LEUKAEMIA RESEARCH FUND

ENERGETIC GAMES

Nell Gwynne's Game   119
EDWINA CURRIE MP

Chocolate Game   119
LEUKAEMIA RESEARCH FUND

Flour Cake Game   120
LEUKAEMIA RESEARCH FUND

Hunt the Kipper   121
ANTON RODGERS

All Change   121
SEBASTIAN COE MP

Make Your Noise, Animal   122
LEUKAEMIA RESEARCH FUND

Mummies and Daddies   123
LEUKAEMIA RESEARCH FUND

The Family Coach   123
DAVID DIMBLEBY

Newspapers on a Train   125
LEUKAEMIA RESEARCH FUND

Soap-savers Game   126
KATHARINE WHITEHORN

Are You There, Moriarty?   127
BROUGH SCOTT

Beating the Plate   128
LEUKAEMIA RESEARCH FUND

11

Coin Game 130
THE RT HON DAME ANGELA RUMBOLD MP

The Obstacle Course 130
LEUKAEMIA RESEARCH FUND

The Balloon Game 131
MICHAEL PARKINSON

Blowing Up the Balloon and Bursting It 131
LEUKAEMIA RESEARCH FUND

Fanning the Kipper 132
STRATFORD JOHNS

Backwards and Forwards 133
VIRGINIA LENG

Bottle Walking 133
STIRLING MOSS

Ball and Spoon Race 134
GUY MICHELMORE

Poor Pussy 135
IAN MESSITER

Pea Picking 135
ALFRED MARKS

Video Fun 136
IAN MESSITER

Guess the Feet 137
JOHN PARROTT

The Sweet Game or The Dentist's Despair 138
ESTHER RANTZEN

LESS ENERGETIC GAMES

The Psychiatrist's Game or Insane Delusions 143
FRANCES EDMONDS
Variation: 143
JOHN JUNKIN

CONTENTS

Crossed and Uncrossed   144
DELIA SMITH
Variation: 144
LEUKAEMIA RESEARCH FUND

Kim's Game   145
SANDY LYLE

This Is My Left Ear   145
IAN MESSITER

Exhausted Tigers   146
LADY VICTORIA LEATHAM

Alibi   147
FIONA FULLERTON

The Christmas Card Game   147
THE MOST REVD DR JOHN HABGOOD,
ARCHBISHOP OF YORK

Family Snap   148
THE RT HON MICHAEL HOWARD MP

The Moose and the Karibu   149
LEUKAEMIA RESEARCH FUND

DIVERSIONS

Blow the Candle Out   155
RUTH MADOC

Round the Room   156
LEUKAEMIA RESEARCH FUND

The Chair Game   156
LEUKAEMIA RESEARCH FUND

The Matchbox Game   157
LEUKAEMIA RESEARCH FUND

Spooning Jelly   157
LEUKAEMIA RESEARCH FUND

Rocket Game   158
LEUKAEMIA RESEARCH FUND

Performing an Operation   158
LEUKAEMIA RESEARCH FUND

The Broom Game   159
DAVID GOWER

Which Book?   159
LEUKAEMIA RESEARCH FUND

Meet Lord Nelson   161
LEUKAEMIA RESEARCH FUND

Athlete and Spoon   161
FATIMA WHITBREAD

GROWN-UP GAMES

The Vicious Dream Game *or* Smile and
    Smile and Be a Villain   165
ADAM NICOLSON

First Night of the Honeymoon   167
NED SHERRIN

A Grown-up Game   167
DEREK NIMMO

Rude Scrabble®   168
CLAIRE RAYNER

Mexicano   168
LEUKAEMIA RESEARCH FUND

Surgeon's Knock   169
JOHN JUNKIN

Index of Games   173
Index of Contributors   175

PUBLISHER'S NOTE

The publisher and the Leukaemia Research Fund would like to thank the many people who were kind enough to contribute to this book, without whose generous support it would not have been possible.

It was inevitable that some very popular games, such as 'The Dictionary Game – with Books' (see page 32) and 'Who Am I? (see page 70), would be chosen by more than one person. In such cases, in order to avoid repetition, instead of printing the contributor's description in full, we have included excerpts which either show variations in, for example, methods of playing that particular game or indicate why the contributor enjoys playing it.

In addition to the celebrity contributors, other people kindly donated games. For these, credited in the book to the Leukaemia Research Fund, we gratefully acknowledge Arianne Burnette, Jenny Dereham, Christabel Gairdner, the late Dr Douglas Gairdner, Captain J.O.H. Gairdner, OBE, RN, and Annie Marsh.

INTRODUCTION

I think that, like many, some of my earliest memories are of Christmas and party games. I remember particularly that very grown-up feeling of being allowed to compete with parents and uncles on equal terms. More importantly, some of those games like 'Charades', in which I did some early acting – may well have been career forming.

Not being allowed, at three years old, to drink a glass of beer while being held upside down and being tickled after the forfeits, I had to opt for an alternative, which was to recite a nursery rhyme to loud and less-than-objective standing ovations.

A decade later, the games had matured. I had put away childish things. As the leading choirboy, I had to organize parties every Sunday, after Evensong. My angel-faced fellow sopranos and I would repair to someone's front parlour, with our faithful groupies, and play the only game in town, 'Torch Solitaire'.

We paired off by drawing lots, and the unlucky odd one out could only get into the game by stabbing a beam of light into the darkness, hoping to catch a couple not kissing, and then take over. Depending on who you were with, you either rather uncharitably got caught very quickly, or kissed the evening away to make sure you weren't. All too soon, our voices broke and our bruised lips healed.

Years later I heard of a country-house game similar to this one. A bed sheet with various holes cut out is held up to divide the separated sexes, who have to identify, through the holes, those on the other side of the sheet. The skill is based on anatomical recognition. You need no torch, but of course someone to hold up the sheet.

The games you will find in this book will provide challenge for all ages, shapes and sizes. When inhibitions and formality are temporarily abandoned, perhaps we get a chance to reach back and touch our childhood. And there is more than a hint of forgotten innocence within these pages. What you should bring to the party is imagination, willingness and laughter – and the greatest of these is laughter.

John Alderton

L aughter was absolutely forbidden when we played 'Dead Horses' at our childhood parties. This game was the parents' secret weapon when things were in danger of getting out of hand.

Everyone lay on the floor not moving a muscle. Not a breath, not a twitch, not a flicker of a smile or you'd be out.

It's curious how even in our grown years, we still want not to be out. I always deny I am a games player, I who have no real desire to win – and yet put me in a team playing 'Charades' or 'Who Am I?' and I become a contender, driven by a fierce team pride. Along with my fellow wrinklies, I become loud and argumentative, quibbling, hysterical and dictatorial.

It's time maybe to reintroduce 'Dead Horses' to my fellow oldsters.

Now everyone lie down on the floor. Still as mice. Don't move a muscle. No twitching. No smiling. You're not smiling, are you? And absolutely no laughing. No laughing! *No laughing!*

Oh well – go on then: laugh, enjoy yourselves!

Pauline Collins

PENCIL AND PAPER
GAMES

CONSEQUENCES

This game is a favourite with my children. Everyone is armed with a pencil and piece of paper. Each player writes at the top of the paper an adjective, folds down his or her piece of paper so what is written cannot be seen and passes it to the player on the left. Each player then supplies a man's name (real or fictitious, or one of the assembled company), folds the paper as before and passes it to the player on the left. The game continues in this way with each player supplying information in accordance with the following convention:

1. Adjective
2. Man's name
3. (met) Adjective
4. Woman's name
5. Where they met and what they were doing
6. He said to her
7. She said to him
8. The consequence was …

As soon as each player has filled in details of what the world said, the papers are folded once again and either passed to the left a final time, or given to an appointed leader to read out. Other things you can add are: 'He wore', 'She wore', 'What he did next', 'What she said …', but we play it like this to keep it simple for small children.

THE EARL OF BRADFORD

THE POETRY GAME

A favourite game played by my friends and family was played like 'Consequences'. Each player had a piece of paper and made up the first line of a poem in an agreed rhythm (di dum di dum di dum di dum); then everyone passed their piece of paper on to the next person who wrote a line to form a rhyming couplet, folded his paper over so that this couplet was hidden, then wrote a following-on line of a new couplet which was passed on again to the next person. He or she then completed this couplet, folded it over, wrote a new line, passed this on – and so on until the various bits of paper were nearly used up, whereupon everyone wrote three lines – one to finish the existing half-couplet and then a complete couplet to round off the poem. Then all the bits of paper were passed on, opened, and the complete poems were read out in turn – as histrionically or dead-pan as one liked.

This may sound a highbrow game, but in fact the funniest lines were nearly always written by people not trying to be literary or too clever but who took their cue from the first rhyme that came into their heads – and the aim was to be funny. I have hardly played this game for forty years, but I still remember the opening couplet of one early poem –

> As I was coming down the road
> I met a stranger covered in woad

– which seemed very funny at the time; I suppose I was quite young, and was pleased with my second line.

My friends and I used to play this game during boring classes in our last year at school. As well as the excitement of not being caught, one of our aims was to write something so funny that when the completed poem was opened the reader, although he could not read it out loud, would be so overcome with laughter that he would have to make out he was having a small fit. And of course, being schoolboys, we could be wonderfully rude.

NICHOLAS MOSLEY

Variation:
Rather than providing rhyming couplets, each player writes two lines of properly scanning verse, turns down the paper over the first line and passes it on to the next player, who writes a further two lines, the second of which rhymes with the line shown on the paper he has received, and so on for as many times as there are players.

THE MARQUESS OF ANGLESEY

LIMERICK GAME

Players sit in a circle, all with paper and pencil, and each writes a suitable first line of a limerick. The paper is folded and passed to the left. The next person writes a word which has to be introduced into the limerick, and passes it on to the left. The next person opens up the paper and has to complete the limerick, using the given first line and compulsory word. Here

25

is an example of one recently – the compulsory word was 'tooth'.

> A curate without any chin
> Found attendance at church growing thin.
> 'Had I even one *tooth*,'
> Said the unfortunate youth,
> 'What hundreds of souls I could win.'

LEUKAEMIA RESEARCH FUND

ADD YOUR OWN LINE TO A FAMOUS POEM'S FIRST

Each player is given a piece of paper and a pencil. All the players together decide on the first line of a famous or pretty well-known poem, then – setting a time limit – you each add your own second line. In turn you read them out for the enjoyment of all. You could vote on which is the best. Example:

> 'The lowing herd winds slowly o'er the lea'
> The leading cow has water on the knee –

or:

> If they were dead, t'would be OK by me.

Example:

> 'Should auld acquaintance be forgot'
> Why ever not? Forget the lot.

LEUKAEMIA RESEARCH FUND

SCRUB A FAIRY

This game is a version of 'Consequences', with a little extra something.

The players are equipped with a pencil and a sheet of paper apiece. Each player begins by drawing a little cartoon or sketch at the head of the paper, and then passes it to the player on his left. The second player writes a caption to the cartoon and the paper is folded over to hide all but the caption, and the paper is handed on again. A cartoon is drawn to fit the caption, which is then folded over to hide all but the cartoon.

And so on, until the paper is covered on both sides. As each paper is finished it is put in the centre of the table. No one may touch the papers until they are all complete.

The special joy of this game, unlike poetry or picture consequences, is that each element refers both ways. Each cartoon is captioned twice, each caption describes two cartoons. The name of the game comes from a particularly imaginative round played between uninhibited old friends. There is no clean way to describe the cartoon that provoked the caption, 'Scrub a fairy'.

ROSIE THOMAS

A EUROPEAN GAME

A game for any number of players, each of whom is given a piece of paper and a pencil. Each player writes down a sentence in English, the simpler the better, then passes it to the player on the right, who translates it (!) into French, folds over the first – English – sentence and passes it to the player on the right, who translates the French into English – and so on. All the translations are then read out, the inadequacy of most people's school French being hilariously exposed. Literal translations are funnier than accurate ones.

CHRISTOPHER MARTIN-JENKINS

LITERARY STYLES

Various topics are decided upon, such as the royal family, keeping goldfish, soap operas, foreign travel, Britain's place in Europe, etc. These topics are written on pieces of paper that are then folded and put into a hat. A sheet of paper and pen is then given to each player, who writes at the top of the paper the name of an author, poet, newspaper, magazine or journalist. He/she then passes the paper to the person on the left, and one of the topics is then drawn out of the hat. Each player then has a set time – say five minutes – in which to compose a short paragraph on the given topic in the style of the writer or journal specified. The literary efforts are then read out – there are no winners as such, the purpose of the game being a source of amusement more than anything, although you could vote on the best effort in each round, with an overall winner at the end of the game.

THE RT HON VIRGINIA BOTTOMLEY MP

THE DICTIONARY GAME

This is a game for any number of players, each of whom is given several strips of paper and a pencil or pen. Player One chooses an unusual word from the dictionary and writes down its meaning on a strip of paper, folds it, then reads the word aloud to everyone.

Each player writes down what they think the word means and passes the (folded) paper to Player One who shuffles all the pieces of paper. He or she then reads out each definition, including the correct one. Each player has, in turn, to guess which of the many meanings is the right one. A score is kept as follows:

· one point for a player who provides the right answer;

· one point for a player whose made-up definition is mistaken for the correct one by another player.

The dictionary is then passed to the next player on the left to provide another word as above. The highest score after a complete round wins.

RUMER GODDEN

Variation:

Our family enjoy playing games at Christmas and other family celebrations. We try to play games that everyone can take part in from the youngest to the oldest and 'Charades' is a firm favourite.

Recently we have played a variation of TV's *Call My Bluff* called 'Balderdash'.

Divide the players into two teams. Each selects several obscure words from the dictionary and writes out definitions for them. One is correct and the others pure imagination. Players give their definitions, elaborating as they see fit, and a player from the opposing team uses their judgement to select the true definition. If the correct definition is chosen, then a point is awarded. If not the point goes to the opposing team.

IAN AND KATHY BOTHAM

THE QUOTATION GAME

This is a variation on 'The Dictionary Game' (see page 29), using a standard book of quotations rather than a dictionary. A group of four to twelve players take it in turns to be in the chair. Writing materials are distributed. The chair selects a quotation from the book, and gives the name and dates of the author to the rest of the players. Each player writes a 'quotation' which might convince the rest that it is genuine. (Not as difficult as it seems, as, of course, the genuine quotation might well be a well-known cliché. However, the more ingenious players will relish the chance of parodying the period of the author.)

After five minutes, the chair reads out all quotations, including the genuine one. Hilarity usually breaks out. After a further reading, a vote is taken. A point is scored a) for identifying the genuine quotation, and b) by those players whose cod quotation is mistaken for the real thing.

SIR IAN MCKELLEN

Variation:
In addition to the points system given above, the questionmaster can also award discretionary points for obscenity, scansion, etc. After each round, the questionmaster changes, one to the left.

SAM LLEWELLYN

THE DICTIONARY GAME – WITH BOOKS

Players are supplied with papers and pens. The first person to go chooses a book and reads out title, author and blurb. The players then write down what they think the first line would be, and hand their contribution in to the person with the book, who has written down the real line.

He/she then proceeds to read out all attempts plus the real one. The participants then vote for what they think is the true line. Scoring is crucial:

· if the real line is not voted for by anyone, the person who chose it gets five points;

· if somebody votes for the real line, they get one point;

· if someone votes for your phoney line, you get two points.

The pleasure and fun of the game is to make the imaginative leap based on the title, plus an attempt at an author's style.

Diana Rigg

Variations:

1. Writing the *last* sentence is either an extension of the game, or an alternative.

Christopher Martin-Jenkins

2. The game is played in much the same way as above, but the reader (the one whose turn it is to choose a book) selects a sentence of not more than eight words at random from the book of his/her

choice and reads out the initial letters of the words. For example, Pepys' *Diary* might render THABSTB (Thence home and being sleepy to bed), or Mrs Beeton's BFBFS (Boil fowl bones for stock). The other players then compose as convincing a sentence with those initials as they can, and write it on a slip of paper. These are collected and placed with the correct sentence and all are read out twice by the reader, in order that the players can guess which of the sentences they believe is the right one. Scoring is as follows:

· two points if you guess the correct sentence;

· one point for every player who wrongly chooses your phoney sentence;

· if a player's sentence is identical with the correct one the reader does not read it out and the player scores five points if he guesses correctly, three points if wrongly;

· if nobody guesses the correct sentence, the reader scores five points.

The game ends when every player has taken their turn to be reader, and the winner is the player with the most points.

SIR JEREMY MORSE

3. The game is a favourite of mine which I was shown by friends during a windswept week on the north coast of Norfolk. It provided hours of entertainment. As a variation you can, after identifying

the actual opening sentence, identify in a subsidiary round which players wrote what.

HELEN ATKINSON WOOD

4. It sounds as though you have to be something of an intellectual to enjoy or be good at the game, but that's definitely not true. You don't. People's imagination can run riot, and you can be as serious or as silly as you like.

CHERYL CAMPBELL

5. Invariably it is not the author's own first sentence that wins, and people's writing styles can often be either very accurate or very funny.

NATASHA RICHARDSON

6. I've found that the adults tend to be too clever and the kids consequently do rather well. The clever people usually outsmart themselves.

It's as well to make clear that Introductions and Prologues do not count; it is the first line/sentence in the main body of the book.

SANDI TOKSVIG

ADVERTISING

Before the party, write out the advertising slogans from a number of products – don't make it *too* easy; include a few obscure ones as well as the instantly recognisable. In addition, cut out some twenty or so advertisements from magazines and newspapers, ensuring that all product names are deleted. Number the slogans and pictures.

At the party give each guest a pencil and piece of paper on which to write all the products being advertised. The winner is the one who correctly identifies the greatest number of products.

DAMON HILL

HEADLINES

Each guest is issued with a pen and paper. A word is chosen at random from a dictionary or book, and each guest then uses the letters of that word (in their correct order) to compose a newspaper headline. For example, supposing the word picked at random were 'economics', the letters might be used to provide headlines such as:

Early Commuter Only Nibbled Old Maid
In Comic Strip

or

European Community Often Narked Our
Ministers In Committee Stages.

Each guest reads out his headline and the others decide who has written the best headline in each round. The winner at the end of the game is the one who has won the most rounds.

THE RT HON NORMAN LAMONT MP

BLIND MAN'S DIP or THE GAME

Outside the room in which you will play the game, fill a white pillow case with as many different shaped objects as you can find which will not break under rough handling. Find objects that are large, medium and small, different in texture and of every shape.

Take the pillow case into the room where the game will be played and make everyone sit in a circle. Give each player a piece of paper and pencil or pen. Put a large clock in a visible position.

Start the game with any player. The player has half a minute in which to put his/her hand in the pillow case (you must keep the neck of it tightly closed, just allowing room to insert the hand). The object is to identify as many objects as possible in the thirty seconds available. He/she must write their answers

down. Generally people put their left hand in the pillow case and write with their right hand. When the thirty seconds are up, the pillow case is passed on to the next person. Keep up the game for as many rounds as players have the patience to endure.

Turn the pillow case upside down in the middle of the room and make everyone check their lists against the real items. Provide a prize for the winner who is the person who has given the longest, most accurate list.

EMMA NICHOLSON MP

BOY GIRL BOY GIRL or THE ALPHABET GAME or CATEGORIES

Each person needs a piece of paper and a pen. The game can be played by as many as you like. Firstly, all the letters of the alphabet are written on separate pieces of paper, folded and placed in a hat. Secondly, each player writes across the top of the paper ten categories agreed by all the players; these may include boys' names, girls' names, cities, flowers, cars, TV programmes, colours, pop groups, books, parts of the body (you can choose others if you like). Then one person (without looking) picks a piece of paper from the hat and reads out the letter on it. You now have two minutes (longer if you all agree) to write something beginning with that letter in each category. At the end of the allotted time, you read out what you have put in each category.

The scoring is simple:

· if you have put something which someone else has also written down (for example, if the letter is V and you have put Volvo for car, but so has your sister) you are awarded five points;

· however, if you have put something which nobody else has got, congratulations, you win ten points. At the end of ten rounds you add up the scores to see who has won the game.

JIMMY MULVILLE

Variation:

I learnt this game from my brother, and we play it so that points are awarded only if no one else has thought of your answer. Some more suggestions for categories include: countries, fruits, trees, jockeys, items of clothing, magazines, animals and films.

ROSEMARY CONLEY

THE DRAWING GAME or PICTIONARY

In my family we play 'The Game' (see page 60) with drawing instead of miming. You have two teams and they either give each other a list of sayings, people, events, quotations, etc., or both teams are given a list, one by one, by some outside judge. Each player receives an item from the list, and has to go back to his/her team and draw it. The others have to guess what it is. Obviously you are not allowed to include either numbers or letters in your drawing, and can only say 'Yes' or 'No' in answer to their questions guessing what it is. Whoever on the team guesses correctly draws the next item on the list, and so on. The winning team is the one that draws and guesses correctly all the items on the list first.

LORD OAKSEY

Variation:

This version is played in exactly the same way as above but uses lumps of Plasticine or Play-Doh instead of a pencil and paper. It's huge fun and rather smutty.

SIMON WILLIAMS

BATTLESHIPS

This is a game for two persons, although more may play. Each person is provided with a pen and a sheet of foolscap or A4 paper – any large blank sheet will do. On this paper each player draws two identical grids of squares, consisting of 11 vertical lines and 11 horizontal lines. Each of these squares will then contain a series of boxes, 10 across and 10 down. The 10 going across should be marked (outside the squares) from A to J inclusive; the 10 going down should be marked from 1 to 10 inclusive. One of the grids is yours, and will contain your fleet of four vessels. The other is that of your opponent. To avoid confusing the grids yours should be identified with your name or HOME, and your opponent's grid with his or her name, or ENEMY. Your opponent will name his or her grids in

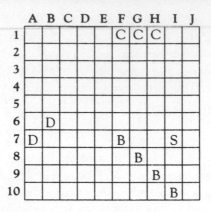

the same way. Each player should of course conceal from the other the piece of paper containing the grids.

You now mark the disposition of your fleet within the grid bearing your name. You each have four squares for a Battleship (mark each square with a B); three for a Cruiser (C); two for a Destroyer (D); and one for a Submarine (S). The Bs, Cs and Ds should be set down in *straight lines* – diagonally, or up and down, or across. They must not abut each other, i.e. a B should not be adjacent to any C, D or the S. There should be a clear square between each unconnected letter. Your Battleship might therefore occupy squares F7, G8, H9, I10, your Cruiser F1, G1, H1; your Destroyer B6, A7; and your Submarine I7.

Decide who will start by tossing a coin. Then each player in turn calls out three grid references – shots aimed at the other person's hidden fleet. Think of them as three random shots (A3, G9, J1), or as a salvo (A2, A3, A4). The other person must state,

40

after each grid reference is called, whether the attacker has scored a *Hit* or a *Miss*.

Both persons should cross off (with an X) on the relevant grids every shot as it is called. The person being attacked need say no more than 'Hit' if a square occupied by a letter (by a B, C, or D) is called. It is up to the attacker to work out by a process of elimination and further shots, *which* vessel has been hit. This of course will soon be revealed in the case of the Destroyer, and instantly if the Submarine is hit. When all the squares marked B, C, or D are hit, the person being attacked will confirm this fact, by saying 'Battleship', 'Cruiser', or 'Destroyer'. You then go on to find and destroy the next ship, each person alternately calling out three shots. When all the squares marking a person's fleet have been hit and each ship totally destroyed, the other person is declared the winner. The papers containing the grids with all the ships, hits and misses marked thereon should then be exchanged, so that these can be verified and the whereabouts of the winner's surviving fleet revealed.

There are variations of this game, but this version is the best. Winning depends on the lucky and intelligent calling of shots, a good assessment of the enemy's thinking, and the careful disposition of one's ships. You could cram all your ships into one half of the grid (without them touching). But a varied distribution is more likely to succeed.

GORDON HONEYCOMBE

OUTDOOR AND
TRAVELLING GAMES

KICK THE CAN

Play this (preferably in the dark) in a big garden or park, with lots of bushes and shrubs. One person is allocated to be the 'finder' and a can or biscuit tin is placed near his base. The finder counts to fifty while the other players hide in the surrounding greenery. The object is for the players to give the can a kick without being caught by the finder. If the finder catches a player (by touching him or her, as in a game of tag), that player must stand by the can and is temporarily out of the game. When a player does manage to break through and kick the can without being caught by the finder, all those temporarily disqualified are restored to the game.

If the finder captures all the players, or when the finder is thoroughly exhausted chasing party guests round the woodland, choose another finder.

IMOGEN STUBBS

Variation:
Instead of kicking a can, a home base is established, such as a tree or a certain room in the house. The players all try to reach the home base without being seen by the finder or 'He'; if this occurs, the caught player has to stand at the home base and shout 'Rescue'. He or she cannot be released until touched by another player, whereupon he or she can rejoin the game. The 'He' is not allowed to hover near the home base once a player does need rescuing as this

45

would prevent any other player approaching the home base and thus stagnate the game.

LUCINDA GREEN

BALLOON TREASURE HUNT

There is nothing my family like better than a treasure hunt, especially at Easter, or if we hold a birthday party in the garden. If there are six people or over, they can divide into pairs for the hunt.

Before the party, hide safety pins in numbered envelopes at strategic points around the garden or house. Put the clues for where the pins are to be

found inside numbered balloons – there should be a balloon at each stage for each person/pair taking part. Each player bursts the first balloon. The clue inside leads to where the safety pin to burst the next balloon is hidden, i.e. pin number two bursts balloon number two and so on.

The first person to reach the last balloon wins the treasure.

WENDY CRAIG

BIBLICAL TREASURE HUNT

We used to have treasure hunts and the clues were biblical 'texts' (not the texts but the references to chapter and verse). We learned a lot about the Bible that way, painlessly.

RABBI LIONEL BLUE

THE BELLMAN

This is a game best played outside, but if you do play it in the house make sure furniture is pushed aside or placed in front of windows, etc.

It's really 'Blind Man's Buff' in reverse: all the players are blindfolded except one, who is given a small bell to ring occasionally as he/she moves among the blindfolded players. The object is for a blindfolded player to grab the Bellman, but of course most of the time the blindfolded players merely grab one another. The player who does manage to seize the Bellman changes places with him.

JOHN TOVEY

A BEACH GAME

This game involves children and is one that's always been enormously popular with my lot. It's ideal for playing on the beach. Each child – and indeed every member of the party including adults – names an object. The more disparate the objects the more interesting the effect. Thus an egg beater; a parrot with no tail feathers; a robin's nest; a lavatory brush – you get the picture. Then the family storyteller (in this family it was Des) has to tell a tale that brings in each one of these objects either in order if that is what is demanded of him or in any order he chooses, in such a way that the story is logical, makes sense, and has a happy ending. It's hell on fathers – wonderful for the listening kids.

CLAIRE RAYNER

GUESS THE PROFESSION

This is a game that we play with our children on long car journeys. It can be varied in difficulty according to the players' ages and is something like 'Twenty Questions' (see page 27). The first player chooses a job/profession and the team has to guess what it is after a maximum of twenty questions to which the answer must be 'Yes' or 'No'. Such questions might include Do you wear a uniform? Do you work with animals/children? Do only men/women do this job? and so on.

NICK AND GILL FALDO

ARMS AND LEGS

Here is a game for playing in the car, to allay the first cries of 'Are we nearly there?' from the children.

You either choose arms or legs. Say it's legs. The passengers on the near side take the pubs they pass on the left, and those on the off side the pubs on the right. Every time you pass a pub whose name qualifies for legs on your side, you add the number of legs to your score. For instance, a pub called the Duke of York scores two, because that's how many legs the dear man had. The White Hart scores four, the Seven Martlets (heraldic birds in Sussex) fourteen; the Anglers four (because there must have been more than one Angler to qualify for pluralisation); the Coach and Horses fourteen (we allow two horses, one coachman and two passengers, but you can decide on your own size of coach); the Dog and Duck six and so on. When you get to a pub (as we did) called the Charge of the Light Brigade, you argue a lot (600 horses, 600 men and a few Russians)! The same rules apply to arms.

LESLIE CROWTHER

CRICKET ON THE MOVE

The game can be played on long car journeys or even in the train for all hawk-eyed players. Basically any time you pass a pub, hotel or restaurant you score runs if you are batting or take wickets if you are the fielding side. Any sign or name of a creature with legs scores one run per leg (e.g. the Red Lion = four runs). Any reference to Sun or Moon scores four runs (so the Sun and Red Cow = eight runs). Any reference to Stars gives six runs (so the Seven Stars scores forty-two runs – whoopee!). Wickets can be taken by any reference to Wheels; the Coach and Horses = probably four wheels and therefore four wickets, but several runs as well depending on the number of horses.

Umpire is the driver and his decision is final. Legs of course can be on inanimate objects such as clay pigeons, tables, etc.; the Farmer's Table would score six runs for the farmer's two legs and four table legs.

An innings consists of ten wickets being taken and then the other side tries to beat the score achieved; you can make it a two-innings game for long journeys.

RACHEL HEYHOE FLINT

DOG SPOTTING

This is a very simple game. Each time someone in the car spots a dog they yell out and score a point. The game ends when a spotted dog is spotted (so to speak), for which you score six points.

ROBERT ROBINSON

THE CAR NUMBERS GAME

For this game it is essential to have a dictionary to hand (for the non-driver). You spot the final three letters of a passing car's number plate, and you have to make those letters in their sequence fit into as long a word as possible. For example, from the registration G364 ADL, the letters ADL can be ADorabLe; AnteDiLuvian; procAtheDraL Score one point for each letter of the word; take one point off if you are unable to spell the word correctly.

CLIFF MICHELMORE AND JEAN METCALFE

NUMBER PLATES

This is a car game and one that is designed primarily to ensure driving parents are left in peace for quite a long way. The passengers have to add up the numbers of the registration plates of cars that are passed (or which pass you!) and collect them in numerical order. Thus the first player to see a car which adds up to the number one starts and then has to find a two and and a three and so on in sequence. For example J886 BBY is a four ($8 + 8 + 6 = 22 = 2 + 2 = 4$: you go on adding the numbers together until you come down to a single digit). The first one to reach nine is obviously the winner and this usually causes loud shrieks and accusations of cheating in the back seat. Never mind – it can give you twenty minutes of children staring hard out of the window and leaving you pretty much in peace.

CLAIRE RAYNER

A STAY-AWAKE GAME

On long watches on moonlit nights, with two in the cockpit, we have evolved a stay-awake game that also works in cars. The crew reads the helmsman one paragraph of Stephen Hawking's *A Brief History of Time*. The helmsman must then explain to the crew, to the crew's satisfaction, what it means. One paragraph should easily occupy four hours, and some will take you across the Atlantic.

SAM LLEWELLYN

THESPIAN
GAMES

CHARADES

This household seems to be very traditional, with 'Charades' high up the list of preferences.

Guests form into two equal teams. Each team has a secret conference to decide on a word containing two or more syllables which will be acted out for the opposing team to guess, and to plan the performance given. Each syllable must have a meaning in its own right, such as lov-able, meal-time, day-trip, table-top, red cabb-age, and including phonetic examples too such as rectorship (wreck, tor, ship), neighbourhood (nay or neigh, bore, hood), herbicide (herb, bee, side) and so on.

The syllables are incorporated within short scenes, acted with words, and the final scene must contain the whole word. So, for example, if the word chosen is 'snowmobile', the first scene might incorporate the word 'snow', the second 'mob', the third 'eel' and the fourth 'snowmobile'.

The opposing team then has to guess the word. If they do so correctly it is their turn to retire and decide upon the word to be acted; if they cannot, the first team retires once again to decide on a new word. The winning team is the one that has undertaken the most performances.

HIS ROYAL HIGHNESS THE DUKE OF KENT

ADVERBS or IN THE MANNER OF THE WORD

Any number of people can play this game. It is essentially an after-dinner game as everyone sits down except for one person who stands outside the door while the rest decide on an adverb. After a heated argument they finally agree on their choice and someone is sent to call the outsider back into the room. He/she may be outraged to find him with his ear glued to the keyhole. Let that pass. The returned outsider then puts a question – any question – to each of the players in turn, such as, 'Why did you choose the dress you are wearing?' or 'Do you like getting up in the morning?' The players have to answer their questions 'in the manner of the adverb' they have chosen: for instance, deceitfully, threateningly, wittily. At the end of each round the outsider tries to guess the adverb. It has to be exactly right; humorously won't do for wittily, nor menacingly for threateningly. When he or she gets it right the next in turn goes out. This game gives great opportunities for histrionic art.

THE COUNTESS OF LONGFORD

Variation:
The outsider has to guess the adverb by asking individuals in the room to perform some action, such as putting a log on the fire, drawing the curtains, taking off a cardigan, etc., in the manner of the word. When the outsider guesses the word correctly, the person whose action gave him the clue goes outside while a new word is chosen.

MICHAEL BUERK

SILENT CHINESE WHISPERS

This is basically the game of 'Chinese Whispers' put in motion, and is funniest if quite a few people play it for reasons which will be obvious. Two teams are formed; one team leaves the room and the other decides upon a scenario which one of the members will mime. Put in quite a few details, and don't simply act out the obvious elements of the scenario. You might consider one of the following to begin with:

washing the car and kicking over the bucket of water;
washing and trimming someone's hair;
cooking and eating spaghetti;
painting a room while pursued by a wasp;
putting a duvet back in its cover.

The first member of the other team is summoned in to watch the scenario being mimed, complete with all its embellishments. He/she then has to mime the scenario as he remembers it for the benefit of the next of his team-mates sent in to the room, who in turn mime the scenario to the next team-mate, and so on until the final team member has to guess what scenario has been acted – by which time it is usually barely recognisable. The teams take it in turns to devise and guess the scenario.

MICHAEL YORK

RHYMING DUMBSHOW

Divide the players into two teams. One team leaves the room while the other chooses a verb – 'sing', 'dance', 'play', 'walk', 'run' or 'jump', for example (as easy choices – but obviously the verb can be as difficult as you like, depending on the ages involved and who is playing). The other team now returns and is told a word that rhymes with the one they have to guess. For example, if the chosen verb were 'hop', they would be told that the secret verb rhymes with 'stop'. The team trying to guess the word now has to act out the word they think it is in dumb show. If they begin to flop about the team hisses, because the verb isn't 'flop'. They hiss at every wrong guess until the acting team start to hop about, when the other team cheers. Teams take it in turns to be the choosers or the guessers.

JANE ASHER

THE GAME

Some confusion exists between 'The Game' and 'Charades' (see page 57), but this is the way 'The Game' is played.

The guests divide into two equal teams. Each team holds a secret conference to compile a list of plays, television programmes, books, films, and songs, including a goodly number of difficult ones such as *Exodus, Flipper, The Mark of Zorro, The Man Who Never Was, How to Succeed in Business without Really Trying, The Harry Lime Theme, Ob-La-Di-Ob-La-Da*.

The guests then reconvene, and a member of one team is given (by whispering or writing down) the title he or she is to mime by the opposing team. The idea, of course, is for that guest to mime the title for his or her team-mates to guess. It's more fun if a time limit of, for example, five minutes is imposed within which the title must be guessed correctly. Naturally no points are awarded if the team cannot guess the title within the given span and any guest who speaks while performing is disqualified.

A member of the opposing team is then given a title to mime for his or her team to guess and so the game continues until all the guests have had a turn. The winning team is the one that has guessed the most titles correctly.

There are a number of conventions associated with The Game. The performer is allowed to indicate from which medium the title is taken by miming the following before beginning:

Book: Hold hands palms uppermost, with little fingers touching like the spine of a book.

Television programme: Draw a rectangle in the air.

Film: Look through the circled fingers of one hand while pretending to crank a camera with the other.

Song: Hold hands to mouth as though calling through a megaphone.

Play: Indicate stage curtains parting in the air.

You are also allowed to indicate to your team-mates the number of words in the title by holding up the appropriate number of fingers before you begin, and using the same device to indicate which word is being mimed during the performance (since the words of the title do not have to be mimed in their correct sequence). Words can be mimed in syllables, and the number of these is indicated by holding the appropriate number of fingers of one hand against the other forearm. Hold up a finger and thumb about half an inch apart for small words such as 'and', 'but', 'so', 'also' and so on.

The word 'the' is given by making a 'T' shape by holding the forefinger of one hand at right angles to the other arm. It's sometimes easier to mime a word or syllable that sounds like the one in the given title; indicate this by tugging your earlobe before miming. If you want to mime the entire title rather than breaking it down into syllables and/or words, show that you are performing 'the whole thing' by throwing your arms wide before you begin.

JANET SUZMAN

Variation:

You play 'The Game' as normal, except that on one person's turn you all agree that when he comes back into the room you won't guess what he's miming. Say, for example, he has been given *The Ascent of Everest.*

He chooses to mime 'scent' for the second syllable of the second word. You all guess as close as you can without actually getting the word – fragrance, sniff, nose, etc.

It's not supposed to be a mean game, but a test of gamesmanship. The fun is in witnessing the frustration of the poor performer. But be careful: one person miming this example grew so frustrated that he climbed the armchair and broke his ankle.

JEREMY BEADLE

THE RETURN OF THE EMPEROR

This is a game for Hallowe'en, though a somewhat complicated one.

You require a darkened flat or house, the stairway or hall lit only by candle or lantern. The guests should be lectured on the solemnity of the occasion by a general in Napoleon's army (use dressing-up clothes), who announces that tonight is Hallowe'en, the one night in the year when Napoleon's corpse is on view. The general leads each of the guests in turn up to the room where the body lies, explaining to them that they can ask three questions only, questions which can be answered by a yes or a no, for on this one night of the year Napoleon is given the power of prophecy.

As the guest is led upstairs, he/she passes the mourning figure of Josephine (suitably attired in tatty ballgown). The room in which Napoleon's body lies is in darkness, the only light in the room coming from the general's lantern. The guest sits on the bed, looks

into Napoleon's face, and asks the questions he/she wants answering. In actual fact, Napoleon's face is a mask strapped on to the feet of an accomplice who lies hidden under the bedclothes, who moves his feet up and down, or from side to side, to give the appropriate response to the questions of his interlocutor. As the guest waits in anticipation for the answer to his/her third and final question, the person under the bedclothes rises up and tries to strangle them from behind.

It is as well to know that small children are less frightened by this game than the adults are. Smelling salts should be kept handy. The joy of the game is that it can be adapted to individual families. It doesn't have to be Napoleon; it could be George IV, Charles II, or the little princes in the Tower (though it may be difficult keeping two small children under the blanket for long enough).

BERYL BAINBRIDGE

I WENT TO PARIS

The guests sit around in a circle and the first player begins the game by saying to the guest on his left, 'I went to Paris', to which the response is, 'And what did you buy?' The first player names an object for which he can provide an appropriate action – he might say, for example, 'A monocle', forming the finger and thumb into a monocle and holding it up to his eye. The second player then says to the player on the left, 'I went to Paris', the third player repeats the response as above, and the second player repeats the first item and gives the action and at the same time performs the action for his own word. So in this case the second player might say 'A monocle' (forming the monocle with the fingers) 'and a wig' (tossing imaginary locks over the shoulders). The game continues in this way, with each player adding an item and action to the shopping list. All the actions must be performed simultaneously, and anyone who is unable to remember all the items, or who cannot perform all the actions at the same time (there's an element of the old trick of patting your head while rubbing your stomach here) is disqualified. The last player to remain is the winner.

WILLIE CARSON

WORD GAMES

WHAT AM I?

I have derived this from a game I produced for many years for the BBC which was the well-known *Twenty Questions*, supposedly invented by Queen Victoria with Lord Palmerston; and it was then known as 'Animal, Mineral or Vegetable'. The game was for the team of (usually) four people to try to find out in twenty questions or fewer what object the questioned person had in mind. The chairman would know the object was, for example, a key ring. He would announce that the object was mineral. After that, members of the team would, in any order, ask questions which could be answered by a 'Yes' or 'No'.

In this version the questioned person has to take on the attributes of the object. For example, the appointed chairman alone knows 'I'm a kettle of boiling water'. The assembled company do not know this. They ask questions which can be answered by a 'Yes' or 'No' or give a choice of alternatives only, e.g. 'Are you indoors or outdoors?' 'Are you sitting comfortably?' 'Would I take you to bed with me?' Instead of limiting the questions to twenty or fewer a time limit of three minutes should be set for each round. If a player guesses correctly within the time limit, that person has scored. The next object is thought up by either the person still guessing when the time is up or by the one who guessed correctly. In this way everyone gets a chance both to play chairman and to score as a team member.

Additional fun can be added by the questioned person thinking he/she is, say, Queen Elizabeth I. If someone wants to do this, it is advisable to look up that person in an encyclopaedia in advance or the questions may be impossible to answer.

Don't fall into the trap of suggesting that the chairman scores when the team fails. This encourages misleading answers from the chair.

IAN MESSITER

TWENTY QUESTIONS or WHO AM I?

Everyone has the name of a famous person – dead or alive – pinned to their back and is not allowed to see who he/she is.

Each player is allowed to ask the others only twenty questions about this person and if he/she doesn't guess their identity correctly within the twenty questions, he/she has to perform a forfeit taken from a box which has been prepared beforehand.

TONY JACKLIN

70

Variations:

1. If a guest receives a negative reply to a question, he/she has to move on to someone else to interrogate. Once the name of the personality has been discovered, the paper is removed from the back of the guest by the person to whom the right answer has been given.

FRED SECOMBE

2. Place the name sticker on the backside of the guests as they arrive at the party. This is one of my favourite games for the children to play at our birthday parties, and is well loved by our friends.

JANE SEYMOUR

3. Each guest at the party writes the name of the famous person on a yellow memo sticker. Taking turns, one person at a time places the sticker on the forehead of another guest. Everyone then has to answer only 'Yes' or No' to the questions asked by the 'stickee', who must try to ascertain whose name is stuck to his/her forehead.

SARAH GREENE

THE HAT GAME

Take as many scraps of paper as there are guests. Mark half of them; put them all in a hat. Each guest takes a piece of paper from the hat; those with the marked pieces form one team and those with unmarked pieces the other. (The game works better with arbitrary teams than it does if you allow people to form natural alliances.)

Each guest is given ten scraps of paper: on each they write the name of a famous – not fictional – person, alive or dead. They fold the scraps and put them in the hat which should now have ten times as many named scraps as there are guests. Each team nominates a timer – somebody with a second hand on their watch – who may play as well as time the other team.

The first team gives the hat to their first player. When the timer from the opposite team says 'Go' the player pulls a name at random from the hat and describes the person named. He/she may use any form of description apart from their name or any part of it. When the team guesses the name the player discards the name, picks another scrap and goes through the process again. If the player either doesn't know the name on a scrap of paper, or doesn't care to use it he/she may put it back in the hat. At the end of one minute the number of guessed names are added up and that score given to the player's team. The hat then passes to the other team. The game ends when the last name is guessed.

NIGELLA LAWSON

IF YOU WERE …

To play this, one person decides to be somebody famous, alive or dead, and tells the group whether it is male or female. Everyone questions that person in turn, but the questions always have to take the form of 'If you were … a flower, what sort of flower would you be?' or 'If you were … a poem, which poem would you be?', etc. The point of the game is to reveal in your answers the essence and personality of the person you have chosen to be. For example, if you were, say, Shirley Temple and you were asked 'If you were a drink, what sort of drink would you be?' you would have to try to think of something sweet, sickly and cute – say, a strawberry milkshake with a cherry on top. I once played this game on a train *en route* to Manchester – and we had some very strange looks when the man I was travelling with kept saying shocking things like 'No I am *not* Marie Antoinette!'

NANETTE NEWMAN

BOTTICELLI

Botticelli is a peculiarly savage form of 'Twenty Questions' (see page 70), suitable for prison sentences or interplanetary voyages. It takes the usual form: one questionee, and a panel of questioners interrogating in strict rotation.

The questionee thinks of a mystery figure, and gives the questioners the initial of the mystery figure's surname. The questioners must then, by close inquiry, determine the identity of the mystery figure.

Assume for demonstration purposes that the mystery figure is Botticelli in person. The questionee announces that the initial is B.

The first questioner might say:

Q: Are you a big shot at the BBC?
A: No, I am not Birt.

The second questioner might then ask:

Q: Are you one of the banes of Bertie Wooster's existence in the novels of P.G. Wodehouse?
A: No, I am not Stiffy Byng.

The questions continue. Should someone ask, for instance,

Q: Are you a constellation mentioned in the shortest of Virgil's *Georgics*?

and the A: (No, I am not Bootes) eludes the questionee, the questioner then has the right to pose a Question Direct, as in:

Q: Are you female?
A: No.

The winner is of course the first questioner correctly to establish the identity of the mystery figure. The successful questioner takes over as questionee.

Variation:

There is a variant game, known as 'Long Botticelli', in which there are no direct questions. Matters follow their usual course, with a challenge system substituted for the direct questions. When a questioner asks:

Q: Are you a painter?

the questionee might reply:

A: Yes, but I am not Frank Brangwyn.

Burning with forensic keenness, the next questioner might ask:

Q: Are you a French painter who was the friend and protégée of Madame de Pompadour and died in 1770?

The questionee may then say:

A: Yes but oh blast I can't remember ... Blotto Bunkhouse Bubbeloni no it's er ...oh, soddit, CHALLENGE.

If the questioner can then supply the information that the artist in question was Boucher, he/she wins the challenge and gets another go.

The questions proceed in rotation as before, the choice of painters being narrowed down as to style and period until after a month or two someone asks:

Q: Did this person live 1445–1510, and was he responsible for the *Primavera* in the Uffizi?
A: Yes, and his name is Botticelli.

SAM LLEWELLYN

75

THE RAILWAY CARRIAGE GAME

This is one of the world's great games, which was played at British spy schools during the First and Second World Wars. Two players are chosen, and each is given a secret phrase or sentence. Adam's might be, 'There is no alternative,' and Eve's, 'You're never alone with a loofah.' Armed with these phrases, Adam and Eve climb into an imaginary railway carriage and converse for five minutes. During that time they each must slip their phrase into the conversation as discreetly as possible. At the end of the journey, which is watched by the rest of the giggling company, Adam must guess what Eve's phrase was and Eve must guess Adam's.

GYLES BRANDRETH MP

PROVERBS

One guest leaves the room and the others, using a dictionary of proverbs if necessary, decide upon a proverb. The solitary player returns and asks questions of each of the other guests in turn. The first to answer must include the first word of the proverb somewhere in his reply, the second player must include the second word of the proverb, and so on. The solitary player may hazard a guess at any point in the game as to what the proverb is, but the maximum number of questions that can be asked is one or two of each guest (depending on the number at the party).

Another guest leaves the room, and so the game continues.

RICHARD BRANSON

WRONG NAME GAME

In normal conversation, and wherever possible, substitute in your sentence the Christian name of a famous person whose surname happens to be that of an everyday object (phonetically or actually). For example:

Diana	=	Dors
Robert	=	Key
Basil	=	Brush
Sir Adrian	=	Boult
Sir Arnold	=	Wine stock
Asil	=	Nadir
John	=	Major
Chris	=	Pattern
Cynthia	=	Pain
Prunella	=	Scales
Wayne	=	Sleep
Sir Robin	=	Day, etc, etc.

To illustrate the possibilities: you might say, for instance, 'What a *Cynthia* the *Sir Arnold* is running low,' or '*Basil* up this mess before you go to *Wayne* and lock the *Diana* with this *Robert*.'

MIN HOGG

TABOO

The first player thinks of a common word that is declared taboo. The word might be, for example, 'the', 'and', 'but', 'so' or 'you'. The player then asks a question of each of the other players, who are disqualified if they make use of the taboo word, or if they hesitate overlong in replying. The answers 'Yes' and 'No' should also be declared taboo to prevent players giving these one-word answers to every question. The last player left answering questions is declared the winner, and chooses the taboo word in the next round of the game.

Variation:
A letter rather than a word is declared taboo, and any player using a word containing the taboo letter in his answer is disqualified.

THE EARL OF YARMOUTH

MONOSYLLABLES

In this game the players are allowed to speak in normal conversation in words of only one syllable – anyone using a longer word must remain silent henceforth. It is actually quite fiendishly difficult to achieve. Variety can be introduced if an appointed leader gives each player in turn a topic upon which to expound monosyllabically – for example, the role of men in the kitchen, the state of the nation, the Olympic Games, train journeys, etc.

THE RT HON THE LORD WILSON OF RIEVAULX

CRAMBO

This was once the most popular parlour game in the British Isles. It was probably invented in the seventeenth century and remained very popular up to the end of Victoria's reign at the beginning of the twentieth century.

One person is appointed to act as timekeeper and scorer. Another person leaves the room while the others decide on a word such as 'viable'. On his/her return the one who left knows that he/she will be given a clue by a word that rhymes with the chosen word – in this case he/she is told 'liable'. He/she might ask, 'Is it "friable"?' 'No.' 'Is it "pliable"?' 'No.' 'Is it "deniable"?' 'No,' and so on until the word is guessed.

The scoring is simple. Five seconds are allowed for the question. If the solo player cannot ask a question within five seconds he/she is out and has ten points added to his/her score. The timekeeper notes the number of questions asked by each person to find the answer and the player with the lowest score at the end of the game is the winner. The timekeeper/scorer should be the next to go out. In that way, everyone gets a chance to play.

Note: A rhyming dictionary is useful, but not essential when planning the game. Beware of words with too many rhymes such as 'admiral – which has, according to my rhyming dictionary, 533 rhyming words; 'bait' has 738. There are others with more.

IAN MESSITER

NUMERICAL PHRASES

Players take it in turns to call out a number, and the first of the other party guests to call out a phrase containing that number is awarded a point. Numbers from one to ten can be called out any number of times during a game, but numbers eleven and above are allowed only once per game. Examples include 'Two...' 'for tea'; 'Three...' 'is a crowd'; 'Four ...' 'leafed clover'; 'Five ...' 'o'clock shadow'; 'Six ...' 'of the best'; 'One hundred ...' 'and one dalmatians', and so on. The player with the most points at the end of the game is declared the winner.

Variation:
Players take it turns to call out a colour. So, for example, you might have 'Red ...' 'sails in the sunset' 'Brown ...' 'study'; 'Blue ...' 'suede shoes', and so on. The points system outlined above applies.

HONOR BLACKMAN

THE TENNIS-ELBOW-FOOT GAME

This family entertainment was used on radio and it usually ends in violence and tears! Someone thinks of a word, any word, and the next person, with no more than a second's delay, must come up with a word that either rhymes or has some connection with it, and so on around the group. Hesitation means you are out, and if your word has no link with the previous one you can be challenged.

MICHAEL ASPEL

Variation:
Since the game must be played at speed, it is best played to the beat of clapping hands to increase the tension. Single words only are acceptable, and the names of commercial products are not allowed, but you can add your own rules too.

CLIFF MICHELMORE AND JEAN METCALFE

POET'S CHAIR

The Poet's Chair is placed in the middle of the room and the party guests sit around it. The first poet sits in the chair and recites a couplet or any line of poetry. The second poet then sits in the chair and recites a couplet or line of poetry that begins with the initial letter of the last word of his predecessor's poem. Example:

First poet:
My heart aches, and a drowsy numbness pains
My sense, as though of hemlock I had drunk

Second poet:
Do not go gentle into that good night

Third poet:
Nymph, nymph, what are your beads?
Green glass, goblin. Why do you stare at them?

The only stipulation is that no line of poetry may be used more than once. Anyone unable to think of a suitable line is eliminated, and the game continues until only one player remains.

Variations:

1. You can either decide a 'batting order' of players beforehand, or award points to the first one to scramble into the chair to recite his or her line(s) of poetry.

2. A harder variation is to stipulate that each succeeding line of poetry must begin with the same word, not just the initial, as the preceding effort. Example:

> *First poet:*
> I knew when Spring was come
>
> *Second poet:*
> Come live with me and be my love.

Third poet:
Love goes toward love, as schoolboys from
   their books.

THE RT HON SIR DAVID STEEL MP

WANDERER'S GAME

This is my adult adaptation of an old and simple children's game.

The assembled company sits in a circle. The game is played clockwise. The first person says, for example, 'I've just come back from Birmingham and I'm going to Midhurst.' The town to which the player is going must start with the last letter of the departure town. The next person in this example, then, might continue, 'I've just come back from Tooting and I'm going to Glasgow.' The next player then thinks of a town starting with W. 'I've just come back from Wrexham and I'm going to Maidstone.' And so on. Failure to follow at once means that player is out. The game gets fast and furious when only two players are left. It is not as easy as it looks.

IAN MESSITER

I LOVE MY LOVE

This game can be found in *Through the Looking Glass*:

   'I love my love with an H,' Alice couldn't help

beginning, 'because he is Happy. I hate him with an H, because he is Hideous. I fed him with – with – with Ham-sandwiches and Hay. His name is Haigha, and he lives –'

'He lives on the Hill,' the King remarked simply, without the least idea that he was joining in the game, while Alice was still hesitating for the name of a town beginning with H.

The next player then follows the formula above, filling a finite number of categories, all of which begin with the same letter of the alphabet. Don't simply go round the players in a clockwise direction, or some of them will work out what letter will be 'theirs' and mentally prepare for their turn well in advance. Instead it's much more fun if there's a leader who calls upon the players at random when a new letter of the alphabet is introduced. Players who falter are eliminated, until only the winning player remains.

Variations:
There are numerous variations on the basic game. One can decide on a finite number of categories to be filled – for example, 'I love my love with an A because [*quality*] he is awkward, because [*name*] his name is Algernon; I will give him [*gift*] an Art Deco lamp, feed him [*food*] on ambrosia and make him a bouquet [*flowers*] of antirrhinums.'

Alternatively, the leader can fire questions at random among the other players, such as 'Why do you love your love?', 'What is your love's name?', 'Where does your love live?', 'What does your love do for a living?'

and so on, the players providing their answers with the given letter of the alphabet, which changes at the discretion of the adjudicator.

Yet another variation has the players providing three adjectives as reasons why they love their loves. For example, 'I love my love because he is accommodating, amusing and approachable', or I love my love because she is bulky, brainy and beplumed'.

PAMELA ARMSTRONG

PRIME RHYMES or STINKY PINKY

The leader thinks of a noun and a rhyming adjective and defines them for the benefit of the other players. For example, 'a foul owl' might be defined as 'a disgusting bird of prey'; or 'old gold' might be defined as 'an ancient precious metal'. These monosyllabic nouns and adjectives are worth one point to the player who guesses them correctly from the definition given, and it is this player who provides the next definition.

Worth two points to the player to correctly identify them are disyllabic nouns and adjectives, such as 'a gory story' (a bloodthirsty tale); 'a simple dimple' (a straightforward dent in the cheek).

Trisyllabic nouns and adjectives such as 'a harrowing farrowing' (a distressing time for a sow giving birth to piglets) or 'a flammable cannibal' (Dr Lecter liable to go up in flames) are worth three points to the first player to correctly identify them.

If none of the other players can correctly guess the noun and adjective being defined, the player providing the definition (and, mark you, it must be properly defined; no cheating) is awarded the one, two or three points as appropriate. The winner is the player who has won most points at the end of the game.

The game is sometimes called 'Stinky Pinky', the noun and adjective of each group being known as a stink pink, a stinky pinky and a stinkety pinkety. The game is played in just the same way as detailed above, with a stink pink scoring one point, a stinky pinky two points and a stinkety pinkety three.

SUE COOK

HOW, WHEN, WHERE AND WHY?

One player is sent out of the room and the other players decide upon a word. The solitary player returns and asks each of the others in turn 'How do you like it?', to which each player gives an appropriate answer. The questioner then asks each player in turn 'When do you like it?' to which each gives a relevant answer. The remaining two questions are similarly phrased and asked of each player and again elicit an appropriate response. The questioner can guess what the word may be at any point in the proceedings, or at the end of the questioning (particularly if the word chosen has a number of meanings – e.g. 'wood' meaning wood from trees; a small forest; fuel for a fire; or a golf club). If, for example, the word might be 'food': the 'How?' might be 'As often as possible; the

'When?' 'At least three times a day'; the 'Where?' 'Out in the open'; and the 'Why?' 'Because it's comforting'.

JAMES HUNT

GHOST

One person says a letter of the alphabet. The next person has to add a letter, without completing a word. So, if the first person said 'i', if you said 'i … n', you'd be out. The only other rule is that you must, if challenged, be able to make a word incorporating the letters you have used. You carry on, with any number of players, until someone can't think of a letter to add without completing a word.

The variant, 'Super-Ghost', allows you to add letters either before or after the existing ones. So, if your initial 'i' has reached, say, 'k … n … i …. f', to add an 'e' at the end would make 'knife' and knock you out. But if you reply 'k … k … n … i … f', you live to fight another day. You'll almost certainly be challenged, because no one will be able to think of a word which includes those letters in that order. 'Jack-knife' does.

JEREMY PAXMAN

Variation:
A scoring system can be introduced as follows. The object of the game is not to finish the word *and* to be the one with the lowest score, either at the end of an agreed time or when one player has scored, for example, thirty points.

87

If a player challenges, believing that the letters given cannot be continued to form a word, he/she has seven penalty points added to his/her score provided the challenged player can say what word he/she had in mind. If, however, the challenged player has been bluffing by adding a letter without having a word in mind, he/she has the seven penalty points added instead.

A player may bluff and claim that the letters can be continued while knowing this to be impossible. If he/she is not challenged within ten seconds all players except the bluffer have five penalty points added.

Also, the player who calls the last letter may declare within five seconds that the word is finished. If indeed it is, he/she has only one penalty point added to his/her score instead of waiting the whole ten seconds and having a penalty point added for each letter there. But if the word is *not* finished and another player can finish it, that player is allowed to add all the missing letters to the end and one penalty point for each letter in the whole word is added to the score of the one who declared the word finished.

IAN MESSITER

GRITTY UVULA

My family love party games and this is one of our favourites. I think it was invented when my brother was a house surgeon at Bart's. It is quite simple, although describing it is a bit tricky!

The idea is to try to think of 26 adjectives beginning with the same letter and place them in front of 26 different nouns, each beginning with succeeding letters of the alphabet. You may not repeat either an adjective or a noun. Famous names are allowed but once you have used a name, e.g. George, you may not use that name again.

To play, everyone writes the alphabet down the middle of a piece of paper. The first player chooses a letter which will begin each adjective – for example, S. Each player then simply places an adjective beginning with that letter in front of each letter of the alphabet, which becomes the first letter of your noun. For example:

Saxon	Architecture
Silly	Boy
School	Concert

The first one to finish, *and* succeed in getting all his combinations accepted, is the winner. It can be maddening, very funny, and occasionally quite rude!

DAME JUDI DENCH

DESCRIPTION SWITCH

Thinking of the present at the time use the *least* appropriate word to describe mutual friends or famous people.

For example: Timid Mrs Thatcher, Petite Cyril Smith, Placid Gazza, Flamboyant John Major, Celibate Warren Beatty, Flabby Lady Di, Macho Prince Edward, Silent Edwina Curry, Statuesque Ronnie Corbett, etc.

MIN HOGG

FRANCES HODGSON BURNETT'S GAME

This game for two to ten players was said to be a favourite of the popular author of *The Secret Garden* and *Little Lord Fauntleroy*. It involves one player standing up and telling the rest what he or she likes and does not like. When one of the players thinks he or she understands the rationale of why this is, he or she raises a hand and gives an example of what he or she thinks the former player likes and does not like. He or she should not explain how the player chooses his or her likes and dislikes. If the second player is right, they are congratulated, and another player has a go. The last player to give an example loses, and has to pay a forfeit (or wash up).

Here is an example. Can you spot what the likes and dislikes are?

I like coffee, but I don't like tea.
I like cabbage, but I don't like cauliflower.

I like green, but I don't like red.
I like boots but I don't like shoes.
I like butterflies, but I don't like moths.
I like bees, but I don't like wasps.
I like football, but I don't like golf.
I like tennis, but I don't like cricket.
I like *Little Lord Fauntleroy*, but I don't like *The Secret Garden*.

All the things I like have a pair of vowels or consonants side by side, but the things I don't like do not include such a pair.

GYLES BRANDRETH MP

AFTER-DINNER GAMES

UP JENKINS

This is an old game, to be played after dinner while the guests sit around the table. They range themselves in two teams on opposite sides of the table, and the members of one team pass a small coin (a 5p piece is ideal) among themselves underneath the table. This obviously calls for a bit of play acting and bluffing while the members of the team pretend to pass the coin to disguise where the coin is really being passed. (Or you can if you wish decide surreptitiously at this point that one person will keep and conceal the coin, while the others carry on pretending.)

At any juncture the leader of the second team can call 'Up Jenkins' and the closed fists of all the first team must be held above the table (naturally with the coin under one of them). The leader calls 'Down Jenkins' and all the team's hands are simultaneously slapped down with palms flat on the table. The other team must now guess under whose hand the coin is concealed – again more bluffing on the part of the members of the team with the coin, as they pretend to fumble with the coin, look sheepish, etc. If a wrong guess is made, the coin remains with the same team to hide again. The second team can proceed with an 'Up Jenkins' again. If the challenge is correct, the teams swap roles.

Variations:
The basic game can be extended by introducing a variety of commands in addition to 'Down Jenkins'. These include 'Aeroplanes', whereby the coin-holding team members make undulating movements of

their hands; 'Tanks', which entails team members making guns with their hands, with two fingers extended; 'Playing the piano', whereby they pretend to play a piano on the table top; and 'Windmills', when players cross their arms with upright hands from left to right and right to left in front of them.

THE RT REVD RICHARD HARRIES,
THE BISHOP OF OXFORD

FIZZ-BUZZ

Players sit around a table or in a circle. The first six players call out the numbers one to six in turn, and the seventh player shouts 'Fizz'. The counting continues around the circle, but any player whose number is either a multiple of seven (e.g. 14, 21, 28) or which contains a seven (e.g. 17, 27, 37) must shout 'Fizz' instead of that number.

In the same way, the word 'Buzz' replaces the number five, its multiples and any numbers containing five. When a number is reached which is a multiple of both five and seven or which contains the two figures (e.g. 35, 57, 70), the player shouts 'Fizz-Buzz'.

Anyone who fails to 'Fizz' or 'Buzz' or who hesitates and fails to maintain the momentum of the counting is out. The winner is the last player remaining.

DR PATRICK MOORE

CLAPPING GAMES

There are many variations of these. Everyone sits round the table clapping in time with each other. Beat both hands on to the table (palms down), clap your hands together. Beat, clap, beat, clap, beat, clap ...

Game one: Each player is allocated a sign – player A might pat his head, B stick out her tongue, C stick his thumbs in his ears and waggle his fingers and so on. The idea is that you pass signals to one another by giving first your signal, then that of another player. So, for example, everyone is beating and clapping in unison as outlined above and player B might start: beat, clap, B's signal, A's signal; beat, clap, A's signal, G's signal; beat, clap, G's signal, A's signal, and so on. If someone does your signal, it's your turn. It doesn't matter whose signal you give after you've done your own – indeed, you will find yourself giving any signal you can remember – but anyone who loses the beat or can't think of anyone else's signal or who forgets their own signal in the heat of the moment is disqualified.

Game two: Everyone is allocated a number (or a colour in yet another variation of the game) instead of a signal, but the game is played in exactly the same way as above, calling out the number insted of giving the signals.

ANNEKA RICE

THE ANIMAL GAME

Each person adopts a miming action that symbolizes a particular animal: for instance, a scissor action with arms for a snapping alligator, a wiggling arm for a worm, tapping for a woodpecker. You take it in turns to 'pass' the symbols. One person starts by making their own signal followed by someone else's. That person has to respond by giving their own signal then another one – but not that of the person who has just signalled to them. If you do something wrong – like fail to see your signal, give a wrong or unidentifiable signal, or hesitate for too long – you are out. Success depends on being able to remember everyone else's signal and having the stamina to keep up when, as animals drop out, the number of participants diminishes and the pace hottens.

LEUKAEMIA RESEARCH FUND

CATEGORY ONE TWO

No equipment is needed for this simple game, in which the players sit in a circle or round a table. A leader is picked who will choose and shout out the first category for which all players have to provide an example without hesitation. The players all together shout 'One, two' between each example given – this gives you a very short time in which to think! The game travels clockwise around the players. An example might be as follows:

Leader:	Japanese cars.
All:	One, two.
First player:	Toyota.
All:	One, two.
Second player:	Datsun.
All:	One, two.

Third player: Mazda.
All: One, two,

and so on, until a player hesitates or cannot think of an example, in which case that player is eliminated. After a disqualification, a new leader chooses a different category.

MIKE GATTING

PING-PONG TABLE FOOTBALL

Everyone sits round the table – the more highly polished it is, the better – and is given a drinking straw. A ping-pong ball is put in the middle and at the signal 'Go' everyone starts to blow down their straws at the 'football'. The idea is to ensure that you keep the ball on the table near your seat but try to make it leave the table near someone else. The person nearest the point at which the ball leaves the table loses a life,

and each player has three lives to exhaust before being eliminated from the game. The winner is the last one playing. Beware giddy spells with this game!

BOB WILSON

MURDER BY WINKING

You need at least six people, the more the merrier, and however many playing cards there are people – one of which must be the ace of spades. You need to be seated so that each person is able to see all the others. Each person is dealt a card, and the person who gets the ace becomes the murderer. He/she tries to wink at one person without being spotted by the others. On receipt of a wink you howl, scream or fall off your chair uttering the immortal words 'I'm dead!' If one of the other players spots the murderer in mid-wink he can challenge and, if correct, wins a point (tallied at the end of the game). A murderer should be able to kill the room with the batting of several eyelids.

DAVID JACOBS

SCISSORS, PAPER AND STONE

The players sit in a circle. On a command 'Go!', or after three thumps with the fist on the table or floor, every player simultaneously holds out a hand in one of the following three symbols: palm flat (representing paper), index and middle finger in a V (scissors); in a fist (stone). Each player is in or out depending on the symbol made by the neighbour on his/her left, in accordance with the following conventions: paper is cut by scissors (so you're out if you've made 'paper' and your neighbour has made 'scissors') but stone can be covered by paper (so you're still in the game if you've made 'paper' and your neighbour has made 'stone'). Scissors are blunted by stone (you're out) but scissors cut paper (you're still in). Stone is covered by paper (you're out) but stone blunts scissors (you're still in). If you and your neighbour make the same symbol you're both still in. The game continues until only one player remains (the winner of the first round) and the second round begins – and so on.

JULIAN PETTIFER

A DICE GAME

This is a silly game for any number of players that my family *always* play on holidays. We invariably finish up falling about laughing and we love it. To play, you need two dice, a pad and a pen or pencil. Across the top of the pad write down the names of the players. You are going to keep score in columns.

A player rolls the two dice and notes the total of the uppermost faces. This can be done only once or as many times as the player chooses to roll the dice. This roll, or set of rolls, is known as a 'round'. However, if the player rolls the dice and one of them has a one (only one dot) on the top, the player loses all of the score built up in that round. For example:

First roll = 6 + 3 (can stop with total of 9 written down);

Second roll = 4 + 2 (can stop with total of 15 written down);

Third roll = 5 + 5 (can stop with total of 25 written down);

Fourth roll = 3 + 1 (has to stop and has no total to write down. Thinks: 'Should have stopped on the last roll!').

But if at any time a player rolls 1 + 1 (two single dots looking up at the player, known in some circles as 'snake eyes') then not only does the player lose the score from the current round but all the score built up on the pad from previous rounds. Very sad, but very funny for the other players. The winner is the first to reach a score of 101.

PAUL DANIELS

CHINESE WHISPERS

This game is best played round a dinner table after copious amounts of wine have been drunk. The first player thinks of a sentence – make it quite a long one, and as absurd as you like. It's a good idea to write it down, too, the message remaining unseen by the other players, of course. The player whispers the message (only once, and as quickly as you can) to the person sitting on his/her left, who then whispers it to the player on the left, and so on around the table until the last player (the one on the originator's right) announces to the assembled company the message in the form in which it has reached him/her. The first player then reads out what the original message was: invariably the two versions bear little resemblance to one another and the final version can be hilarious.

The next player then thinks of another message to be whispered from player to player around the table, and so on.

LYNDA BELLINGHAM

CARD GAMES

SPOONS

A game that can be played with any number of people, the more the merrier. Take from a pack of cards the four suits of however many numbers there are people playing. Shuffle the selected cards and deal out four cards to each person. Everyone sits in a circle, in the centre of which you place a pile of spoons, one fewer than the number of people playing. When someone says 'Go!', everyone puts down one card to their left and picks up one card from their right; and keeps doing so until someone has collected four of a kind in their hand. Whereupon they immediately shout 'Spoons!', and everyone has to grab one of the spoons in the middle. Whoever fails to get a spoon is out.

For the next round, remove one set of four cards and one spoon. Carry on playing until there is one person left, the winner. With large numbers of people this is best played on the floor: it is likely to degenerate into quite a physical game with everyone flinging themselves about, desperately grabbing spoons.

FELICITY KENDAL

PAIRS

A pack of cards is spread out face down on the floor or tabletop. The first player turns up two cards. If they do not form a pair – two aces, two threes, two kings, etc – he/she turns them over so they are face down again, and it is then the turn of the player on his/her left to turn over two cards. When a pair is turned up, the player removes those cards from the game and is entitled to another go. After the first few rounds the positions of certain cards will have been established, and the players who have a good memory and/or have been paying most attention will remember where they are and consequently be able to pick up most pairs. When all the cards have been removed from play, the winner is the one who has collected the most pairs.

COLIN COWDREY

SHOP SNAP

This game can only be played by consenting adults, children and anyone approaching my own degree of silliness.

You'll need a pack of cards, or if there are a lot of you, two packs. Prior to the game, each person chooses a shop to own. This can be, for example, a sweet shop, a grocery shop, a butcher's shop, a pet shop, a wine shop or, my children's favourite, a sex shop. You then proceed to play ordinary snap, whereby each player lays down a card in turn (in a pile in front of them) from their pile. Should two people find they have the same card, it is their duty, not to yell 'Snap", but to ask the other person for an item from their shop before the other person does the same.

Sounds easy, yes? All you have to say is, for instance, 'I'd like a pound of margarine, please' to the other person if he/she owns the grocery shop. However, the fun comes from the fact that you cannot remember your opponent's choice of shop, you cannot remember your own choice of shop and you usually find yourself shouting wild, mindless obscenities in order to prevent the other person speaking at all, let alone asking you for an item from your shop.

Call me intellectual if you must, but this is one of my very favourite ways of passing an evening.

MAUREEN LIPMAN

Variation:
Another version of this game is 'Animal Snap'. Instead of owning a shop, each person adopts an animal noise. If you put down the same card as someone else's, you have to make the other person's noise – if you can remember what it is – before they make yours.

LEUKAEMIA RESEARCH FUND

CHEAT

This game can be played by three or more people. The entire pack of cards is dealt equally among the players with any left over placed face down in a pile in the middle of the table. All the players examine the cards they have been dealt, and the player on the dealer's left begins the game, laying a card face down on the pile of leftover cards (if any) and calling out its denomination e.g. 'eight'. The player on his or her left must follow in numerical sequence, laying a card face down on the pile and calling 'nine' – though if he/she has no nine in his hand, he/she cheats by putting down a card of any denomination and hoping that he/she can get away with it. It is also possible to cheat by laying down more than one card. The game continues in this way, with the ten followed by the jack, queen, king, then ace, which in turn is followed by two.

At any point any player can accuse another player of cheating by shouting 'Cheat!'. The last card played is then turned up and if indeed the accused *has* cheated then he/she must pick up all the cards in the pile. If, however, the accused player has played a card honestly, it is the accuser who must pick up all the cards. The player on the left of the accused then begins the game with a card of his own choice. The first player to play all his/her cards is the winner.

GARETH HUNT

OLD MAID

A pack of cards is shuffled thoroughly and one card – no one must see what it is – is discarded and placed face down in the middle of the table. All the remaining cards are then dealt, and the players examine them. Each player then discards any pairs he/she holds in his hand – two queens, two fives and so on. The player on the left of the dealer offers his/her hand, face down, to the player on the left, who takes one card and looks at it. If it forms a pair with another card he/she already holds, he/she discards them. This player then offers his/her hand, face down, to the player on the left, who picks a card, and so on round the table.

Eventually all the cards will be paired and discarded, leaving one player – the Old Maid – with the card that is the pair of the one that was placed in the middle of the table at the start of the game. The Old Maid must then pay a forfeit.

RORY UNDERWOOD

CABOOSH

1. Caboosh is a card game for an even number of players, preferably six in number or more although four can play. The players are split into two teams of equal size, and players from each team sit alternately round the table. Aces are low.

2. Take three or more packs of cards and shuffle them together. Deal/divide these cards into 'dollops' of four cards and place a set of dollops face down at each corner of the table.

3. Take another shuffled pack of cards and divide it into two equal half-packs (or 'demons') and place these face upwards in the middle of the table.

111

4. Each player takes one dollop of four cards. One player takes charge at this stage by asking each player in turn, starting with the player on his immediate left and continuing in the same direction, if he has an ace. A player holding an ace must declare it and the first player to declare an ace becomes the first to play.

5. The first player chooses which demon will be his team's demon. He/she will normally choose the demon with the lowest card on top since this can be played earlier.

6. (a) Cards are played face up on to the table in piles, regardless of suit, in the order Ace, 10, J, Q, K.

   (b) A player can play from:
       (i)   his own team's demon
       (ii) the dollop in his hand
       (iii) his own tabled cards or (see 7b)
       (iv) the tabled cards of other members of his own team.

112

(c) A player may *not* play from:

    (i)   the opposing team's demon

    (ii)   the opposing team's 'tabled' cards.

(d) If a player can play, he must. If he can at any stage play from his own team's demon he must do this in preference to any other move.

7. The first player commences play by playing:

(a) the top card from his team's demon, if this is an ace; and then

(b) the ace in his dollop which he has declared.

He can also play any other ace in his dollop but he must play any other available cards from his team's demon or from his dollop in rising sequence. When he can play no more cards, he places one card from his hand face upwards on the table in front of him saying 'Tabled' – this signifies the end of that player's move.

8. (a) Each of the other players in turn, clockwise, plays either aces, or cards in sequence on the top of cards which have already been played, playing cards first, if he can, from his own team's demon as explained in 6 (a) and (b) above. Each player finishes his turn by tabling a card face upwards in front of him saying 'Tabled'.

(b) No player may be helped in playing by winks or kicks, etc. by a member of his own team.

9. Each player's tabled cards are placed face upwards in a row at the edge of the table in front of him

and kept clearly segregated from cards that have been played, which should be kept in the middle of the table. When a player has four cards so tabled, any subsequent cards he tables must be placed face upwards on one or more four cards so tabled so as to half cover the card(s) underneath. A card so covered can nevertheless be played by that player or another member of his team if it becomes exposed by the card on top of it having first been played. A card once tabled can only be disturbed in order to play it.

10. When a player has played, or tabled, all four cards in his dollop he picks up another dollop. If this happens before he has tabled, the player must say 'Still in play' as he picks up his new dollop.

11. (a) Any infringement of the rules by a player may be challenged by a member of the other team by saying 'Caboosh!' If 'Caboosh' is validly called, the bottom card from the demon of the challenging player's team is moved to the bottom of the other team's demon.

(b) Commonly called infringements are:
   (i)   failing to play from your own team's demon when you can do so
   (ii) playing from the other team's demon
   (iii) playing a card in incorrect sequence or failing to play when you can do so
   (iv) failing to say 'Tabled' when tabling or 'Still in play' when picking up a fresh dollop while still in play

(v) running out of time, when playing with a time challenge system in force (see 12 below)

(vi) incorrectly 'Cabooshing' another player

(vii) receiving help in playing from a member of your team

(viii) 'shilly-shallying' – hand changing direction or withdrawing

(c) A player who is successfully Cabooshed must immediately stop his current play and table saying 'Tabled' and the next player commences immediately.

(d) 'Caboosh!' must be called promptly

12. Once players are reasonably experienced a time challenge element can be introduced. When this system is in force, the opposing team, if it considers that an opponent is taking an unreasonable time in play can chant, preferably in chorus, quite slowly, 'One – two – three – four – five – six – seven – eight – nine – CABOOSH!', and if the offending player has not played or tabled a card by then his team suffers the penalty appropriate to a 'Caboosh!' (see 11(a) above).

When he so plays or tables a card in time the challenge fails but the calling team is not penalised. Although the offending player may be time-challenged again in the same turn the whole point of the system fails if time challenges are made too frequently or as a matter of course. *Note:* It has been known for time challenges to be used for slightly intimidatory purposes at critical

115

points, more particularly towards the end of a game.

The game ends when one team has got rid of their demon.

LEUKAEMIA RESEARCH FUND

ENERGETIC GAMES

NELL GWYNNE'S GAME

The party guests stand in a circle and pass an orange from one to another, holding the orange under their chins. Players who drop the orange or who cheat (by attempting to use hands, for example) must leave the circle. It should only be undertaken by people who know each other well – or intend to – and is not advised after a meal involving curry or garlic.

Variations:
There are a number of versions of the game. These include passing the outer casing of a matchbox (pocket size, not household!) from the end of one player's nose to the next. Or pass along a piece of cooked spaghetti, making it shorter as it gets passed on. And there's a trickier version which involves passing a balloon held between the knees from one player to another.

EDWINA CURRIE MP

CHOCOLATE GAME

Before the party, place a bar of chocolate in the refrigerator and gather together a selection of old clothes (including a large pair of gloves). You will also need a knife and fork.

To play the game, everyone rolls a die until someone gets a six. That person then has to dress up in the old clothes (which have been placed in a pile on the floor in the centre of the circle of people), put on the gloves, pick up the knife and fork and begin eating the chocolate, which they must cut up square by square. Meanwhile, the others carry on taking it turns to throw the die. The object is for the person in the old clothes to eat as much chocolate as possible before the next person gets a six. The second person has to do the same thing – after the first has taken off all the old clothes, of course. The first person returns to the circle of throwers. The game continues until all the chocolate has been eaten.

LEUKAEMIA RESEARCH FUND

FLOUR CAKE GAME

Before the party, pack flour tightly into a mould then turn it out on to a plate to form a kind of cake, on top of which is stuck a Smartie.

To play the game, players take it in turns to throw a die. When someone rolls a six he/she has to cut into the flour cake with a knife (one cut only), then the next person to roll a six does the same, and so on until the Smartie falls off the top. Whoever causes it to fall then has to retrieve it without using their hands. One of my cruel friends used to have everyone go bobbing for apples before they played this game, just so they were all good and wet!

LEUKAEMIA RESEARCH FUND

HUNT THE KIPPER

Before the party the host or hostess places, say, twenty objects around the house. Camouflage is of the essence here: the items must all be in sight, not hidden in cupboards or under rugs or whatever, but must not be placed in immediately obvious places. So, for example, you might stick a small round sticking-plaster on an orange in the fruit bowl; shove a pencil in a plant pot with a leafy occupant; lay a match along a skirting board, and so on.

The host or hostess then provides each guest with a list of the items to be hunted, stressing that they mustn't make it obvious when they have seen any of them. Guests should all be aware that the items are in sight, or all sorts of embarrassing things might be unearthed as they rummage in the bathroom cabinet, in the darker recesses of the cupboard under the sink or among the fluff under the sofa.

The first guest to have correctly spotted all the objects is the winner.

ANTON RODGERS

ALL CHANGE

The players stand in a circle and each is given an object to hold. These should be as different in size, shape and weight as possible, and might include the following: an orange, a needle, a brick, a glass of water (outside use only!), a 5p piece, a broom, a raw egg (or a hardboiled one, but don't tell anyone it's cooked), a lady's handbag, a bunch of flowers, a pillow.

A leader is appointed to call out instructions, the first of these being to designate two or three of the objects as special cases. The leader shouts 'Go!', whereupon each player passes the objects in a clockwise direction, with the exception of the special objects, which are passed anticlockwise. At irregular intervals the leader shouts 'All change!', whereupon the objects must all be passed in the opposite direction to the current one. Any player who drops any article or who passes an object in the wrong direction leaves the circle, but all objects remain in play. The winner is the one who ends up holding all the objects.

SEBASTIAN COE MP

MAKE YOUR NOISE, ANIMAL

Children and adults alike seem to revel in this game.

One team outside the room, the other within. The team within decides on an animal noise they wish one of the outside team members to make, e.g. a pig, and shout 'Ready' when they've so decided. Enter one outside team member, under a blanket and taking care not to let any part of the body show. Chorus from inside team: 'You are a pig. Make your noise, animal,' and the person under cover responds appropriately. The team inside has to guess who it is grunting/squeaking under the blanket. Gain a point or lose one accordingly. It's best done on the basis of the first team to lose three lives, or similar, i.e. if you guess the animal under cover, the opposite team loses a life, etc.

LEUKAEMIA RESEARCH FUND

MUMMIES AND DADDIES

Each guest is (confidentially) given the name of an animal. Everyone is either a mummy animal, a daddy animal or a baby animal, and there is only one mummy, daddy or baby of each kind.

At the command 'Go', everyone has to start making the noise of their animal and try to find the other animals in their family. So if you are a baby pig, you have to go round oinking until your mummy or daddy hear you, or you hear them. When the family is united, mummy animal has to sit on daddy animal, and baby animal has to sit on top of mummy animal. The first family so united is the winner. This can be quite a good 'getting-to-know-you' game at the beginning of a party.

LEUKAEMIA RESEARCH FUND

THE FAMILY COACH

This is the Christmas game we loved most as children. A game for up to thirty players of all ages, it is based on a story. A princess is leaving her palace to cross the mountains to wed her prince. She sets off in the family coach with footmen and outriders and a dog running between the wheels. Crossing the most dangerous part of the mountain pass, the coach is waylaid by highwaymen. The family are all ordered out of the coach at the point of a pistol. The bravery of the prince who has come anxiously looking for his bride-to-be saves the day. The highwaymen are arrested and the family coach makes its triumphant progress to the wedding.

There are any numbers of variants to this story and it does not matter much what story is told as long as it is sufficiently enthralling to make the players forget their parts and so give a forfeit.

There are three simple rules:

1. Each player is given a role to play: the prince, the princess, the king, the queen, the nurse, the footmen, the coachman, the highwaymen, the horses, the wheels, the dog. The list is limitless and can with ingenuity be extended to give every player their own part. If there are too many players you may end up having front wheels and back wheels, or first footman and second footman.

2. Whenever one of these names is used in the story the relevant player must stand up, turn around and sit down again. Failure to do so leads to a forfeit being placed in the middle of the room.

3. At the words 'family coach' everyone has to get up, turn round and sit down.

The skill rests with the storyteller, who has to begin quite slowly, making sure everyone knows their name and has a turn, and then gradually speeding up until at breakneck pace the family coach hurtles down the mountainside to the prince's palace with the players leaping up and down like yo-yos and shouting 'Forfeit' at each other.

After an exhausting fifteen or twenty minutes the story ends and the forfeits have to be reclaimed, providing the usual chance to embarrass members of the family or hear children perform ghastly pieces on the piano or haltingly delivered poems.

It is important to have a confident storyteller, who should write down the names of all the players and their parts so that no one is left out in the drama. It is also wise to jot down some forfeits in advance as there is nothing worse than thinking them up under pressure at the last moment. If your family is anything like ours was, your greatest difficulty will be preventing the extroverts making deliberate mistakes so that they can show off at the end. Be tough on them.

DAVID DIMBLEBY

NEWSPAPERS ON A TRAIN

Six, or preferably eight, people sit huddled in two rows, knees close together as in a crowded railway carriage. Each is given a copy of a broadsheet newspaper such as *The Times* or the *Daily Telegraph*, the pages of which have been hopelessly muddled: some upside down, some back to front, all in the wrong order. At the word 'Go!' everyone tries to get the papers in the right order disregarding the efforts of the passengers next door and opposite.

At a suitable moment another passenger enters and passes down between the knees of the players, wreaking the maximum of havoc to their efforts with the papers (a typical experience). Pandemonium can be guaranteed. The winner is the first one to get his/her paper in order.

LEUKAEMIA RESEARCH FUND

SOAP-SAVERS GAME

In my family we used to play such games as Racing Demon, or pencil and paper games like 'Categories' (see page 37). The main fun was watching one's blameless, and indeed saintly, grandmother cheating like a fiend in order to win points.

But the game I remember most fondly is one I invented myself for my own children. You need at least six of those oval soap-savers which are made of rubber and have suckers along one surface like an octopus; a fairly tiled or glossily painted bathroom, and an assortment of children not much more than ten divided into two teams. Each team has a go at throwing their soap-saver up the wall and the people who get them highest win. Points are deducted for hitting the ceiling, hitting each other or actually breaking anything in or out of the bathroom medicine cabinet.

I first thought of it on a wet afternoon in desperation, but it became a family staple and highly popular at parties. Whether I shall have the energy or the nerve to pass this on to my own grandchildren, only time will show.

KATHARINE WHITEHORN

ARE YOU THERE, MORIARTY?

A well-known but nevertheless very popular game, for which the equipment is minimal: you simply need two rolled-up newspapers (broadsheet rather than tabloid are best) and two blindfolds. Two blindfolded players lie on the floor, face down, each grasping the other's left wrist in the left hand, and a rolled-up newspaper in the right. The first player asks 'Are you there, Moriarty?' to which the second must reply 'I am here' before rolling or sliding out of the way while the first player attempts to hit him/her on the head with his newspaper. An adjudicator decides whether the questioner has scored a direct hit or a miss, and so the game continues, with the two players taking it in turns to either ask the question and take a swipe, or to supply the answer and attempt to avoid the blow. The player who strikes the most blows is declared the winner; alternatively the one with the fractured skull is deemed the loser.

BROUGH SCOTT

BEATING THE PLATE

One member of the party goes out of the room, and the others decide what actions he is going to be made to perform. That decided, one person begins to beat a plate with the back of a fork. It is a continuous movement, just a gentle noise when the outsider is called back into the room. The plate is thereafter beaten hard or gently according to how well the outsider is doing, in a sort of hunt-the-thimble/getting warmer ploy.

For example, you might decide that the outsider is to come in and take off both shoes and one sock. Then, taking a rose from the bowl of flowers and putting it between his teeth, he will cross the room to a certain pretty young lady, take off her shoe, put on his own sock, then put the rose in the shoe and present it to her.

When the outsider comes in he will, if he is experienced at the game, start by touching either himself or each person in the room. When he touches himself the plate beat should be vigorous. He will then run his hand over himself, the plate-beat gentle, until he reaches his feet, when the plate is beaten hard; he knows, therefore, that the action has something to do with his feet/shoes. He will take off one shoe – lots of noise; the other – lots of noise; the plate beater must then reduce the noise again until a sock comes off; reduce again and continue muted if the second sock comes off to tell the player that action is wrong. The player then has to find out what to do next; again, the experienced player will touch each member of the party, but at this stage the plate-beat must remain muted. He should then travel round the room touching furniture etc; when he gets near the flowers the beat should increase, and so on until the player has reached the end of the actions to be performed.

It is best to choose actions that are not too long or complicated, and it is as important to have a good plate beater as it is to have someone who is prepared to play the game fast and inventively; like 'The Game' (see page 60) this is hopeless when the player stands in a heap saying 'I don't know what to do next.' The actions to be performed can be varied according to age of player, time of evening and alcohol consumed. A woman climbing into a pair of men's trousers and doing a handstand against the bookcase is an interesting one. We were brought up on the story of the game being played by a very fat friend of my parents, stripped to his underpants and socks (and I expect his suspenders), wriggling under a rug on the floor.

LEUKAEMIA RESEARCH FUND

COIN GAME

The game played at our New Year's Eve party which was very successful was where you have to walk from one end of the room to the other with five 2p coins held between your knees and drop them into a tankard at the other end. This is played in teams and the team with the largest number of coins collected is the winner.

THE RT HON DAME ANGELA RUMBOLD MP

THE OBSTACLE COURSE

For this game you need a fair-sized room and enough people to make a good audience, with one or two to leave the room and provide amusement for those left inside. There is no competitive element in this, it is just a bit of fun at the end of the evening.

Send two or three people out of the room. Those left inside then lay out some sort of obstacle course, a chair here, a sheet of newspaper there, a few cushions on the floor, a small table you could crawl under, and together you plan what you'll ask him/her from outside the room to do, blindfolded. Bring in one of those outside, *not yet blindfolded*, and demonstrate the course: for example, walk round chair, step over newspaper, crawl under table, hand someone a magazine from the top of the table or whatever. He/she then leaves the room and very quickly you remove all the obstacles. Bring the victim in again, *now blindfolded*, and the hilarity begins as he/she treads so very carefully over,

130

round and under nothing. They then join those inside while the process is repeated with the other victims.

You cannot do many rounds, since those outside, hearing all the laughter, begin to wonder what's going on, but certainly you can enjoy two or three people doing it.

LEUKAEMIA RESEARCH FUND

THE BALLOON GAME

Each player is given a rolled newspaper and a balloon with a long piece of string attached to it. The balloon is tied to the player's ankle and each player then tries to burst the other players' balloons with the newspaper, at the same time thwarting the other players' attempts to destroy his/her own. When one's balloon is burst the player retires to watch from the sidelines – it's almost as much fun to watch this game as to play it, in fact. Cheating in the form of using anything other than the rolled newspaper to burst your opponents' balloons is to be abhorred, of course. The winner is the last player whose balloon has not been burst.

MICHAEL PARKINSON

BLOWING UP THE BALLOON AND BURSTING IT

Place two chairs parallel to each other at one end of the room and assemble the guests in two teams

at the other. In turn, each member of the team has to
speed to the chair, pick up a balloon, blow it up, fas-
ten it, sit on it and burst it. Speed back, then the next
person does same. The winning team is the first
whose members are all home having blown up, sat on
and burst their balloons.

Handy hint: be brave and blow big else it won't
burst.

LEUKAEMIA RESEARCH FUND

FANNING THE KIPPER

Each player is given a 'kipper' cut out of newspaper
and a newspaper or magazine with which to fan it.
A starting and finishing line is established, and the
players line up with the tails of the newspaper kippers
touching the starting line. The starter yells 'Go!' and

each player has to waft his/her kipper to the finishing line without touching it in any way with the newspaper or magazine or indeed with anything else. The winner is the first kipper across the finishing line.

STRATFORD JOHNS

BACKWARDS AND FORWARDS

The guests form pairs – encourage married couples to avoid pairing up together – and, standing back to back, link arms at the elbows. Each pair then assembles at the starting line, one of the partners facing forwards and the other backwards. They all race to the far end of the room (or the garden wall, if the race is being run outside), then race back with the formerly backward-facing partner now facing forward and the partner now facing backwards. The first pair back to the starting-line are the winners. It's not as easy as it sounds.

VIRGINIA LENG

BOTTLE WALKING

Push all the furniture to one side or, better still, play this game in the garden. Each player is given two empty beer bottles and a straight line is established on the ground, using a length of tape or string, a garden cane secured at either end, or similar. Keeping both feet behind the line, each player takes a

133

beer bottle in either hand and 'walks' on the bottles, stretching along the ground and taking 'steps' with each bottle alternately. When he has reached as far as he can without allowing his feet to overstep the straight line, he leaves one of his bottles there and hops back to the starting line on his remaining bottle, using both hands, without allowing any part of his body to touch the ground. Anyone who is unable to hop back to the starting line is disqualified, and the winner is the player who has left his bottle furthest from the line and successfully hopped back.

Since men are in the main taller than women and therefore able to reach further, it is best to divide the party guests into male and female teams.

STIRLING MOSS

BALL AND SPOON RACE

The guests divide into two teams and form into two lines. Each player is given a spoon, the handle of which is placed in his/her mouth. The first person in each line is given a ping-pong ball to place in the bowl of his/her spoon.

On the command ' Go!', the players pass the ping-pong ball along the respective lines by means of the spoons held in their mouths, without touching the ball with their hands. If the ball is dropped it must be picked up using only the spoon held in the mouth. If any handling takes place, the ball has to go back to the beginning of the line once again. The winning team is the one that gets the ball to the last player in the line without touching it other than with the spoon held in the mouth.

GUY MICHELMORE

POOR PUSSY

The assembled company sits in a circle, preferably on the floor, determined not to smile or laugh. Whoever is chosen as Pussy must walk on all fours round the inside of the circle looking each player full in the face. Now and then Pussy stops and says 'Miaow!' to the nearest person. That person must say 'Poor Pussy'. At the next stop Pussy says 'Miaow!' twice. That person must say 'Poor Pussy' twice. At the next stop Pussy miaows three times and the player thus faced must say 'Poor Pussy' three times; and so on, but not for long as sooner or later everyone laughs. When a player laughs or smiles he/she is out.

IAN MESSITER

PEA PICKING

A family game that requires a minimum of equipment: only a pair of chopsticks, a small bag of frozen peas and two bowls. Place all the peas in one bowl, and reveal to your guests that the object of the game is to pick up the peas with the chopsticks and transfer them to the other bowl, within an agreed time limit. If there are any members of your party renowned for their dexterity with chopsticks, they should be given only half the time allowed, or perform the feat with the chopsticks in their left hands. The winner is the one who can shift the most peas within the time limit.

ALFRED MARKS

VIDEO FUN

As personal video cameras are appearing in many households it seems sensible to invent a game for them. For the game you need a video camera, television set and wires to connect the video camera straight to the television set. You will also need a length of ribbon and a man's neck tie (a bow tie if you like), and a stopwatch or wristwatch with a second hand on it.

The camera is mounted on top of the television set and pointed directly at the player who faces the set. The player's mind says he/she is looking into a mirror even though he/she knows it is not a mirror. Contestants are timed as they take it in turns to perform the following actions while watching what they are doing on the screen. Females must put the ribbon round their neck and, watching the television screen, tie a bow over the Adam's apple. Males must tie either a normal neck tie or a bow tie. The one who can do it fastest is the winner.

Variations:
1. Try drawing a simple house (roof, walls, a window

on each side of the front door and three windows above with a chimney on the roof). The *inverted* camera is pointed at the drawing paper, which has a tree drawn on it to show which way is up. A tray is held between the artist's face and the paper so that the artist is unable to see anything but the television screen showing a picture of a tree *the right way up*. People get into absurd muddles.

2. This is another way to make a fine mess of the paper. Before the party, draw a grid of squares six by six. Fill them with numbers one to thirty-six in a haphazard fashion (in other words square two must not be next to square one, etc.). Make as many photocopies of the grid as you have players.

   To play the game, use a tray to stop the player seeing anything except the television screen. Invert the camera as in the first variation above. The player must draw a pencil line from square one to square two, and from two to three, three to four and so on until he/she reaches square thirty-six. The company vote for the paper that is best done with fewest lines showing where the player was sidetracked.

IAN MESSITER

GUESS THE FEET

The players divide into two teams – arbitrarily, or ladies/ gentlemen, it's up to you. One team leaves the room while the others remove their shoes, socks, tights, whatever and stand or sit behind a screen – an old blanket held up by two non-players provides a good one – with only their feet and ankles in view. The opposing team then re-enters the room and makes a list of which feet they believe belong to which guest. The team then change places. The winning team is the one that has correctly identified the greatest number of feet.

JOHN PARROTT

THE SWEET GAME or THE DENTIST'S DESPAIR

This is suitable for children aged eight and under, though I have known a child of fifty-six play it with pleasure.

The children all sit on the floor round a cloth, scattered on which are many different kinds of small sweets such as fruit pastilles, Smarties, chocolate buttons and the occasional wrapped chocolate sweet.

Each child is given a paper bag, and the children are then numbered in order. The first one goes out of the room and has to promise not to listen after the door is shut. The child last in the numbers then nominates the sweet which is going to be 'it'. The first child then comes back into the room and takes one sweet at a time, putting them into the paper bag. As every sweet except 'it' is picked the audience shout 'Yes'; when the child reaches 'it' the audience shout 'No' and that child's turn is over. A very important rule is that even when the child takes 'it' he/she can keep 'it', otherwise it is possible for a child to end up with no sweets at all if they choose 'it' first.

Every child takes it in turn to pick the sweets. Clever psychologists can tell from the confidence of the 'Yes' how close they are to 'it' and can therefore skirt their way round it and take it last, in which case they have swept the board.

ESTHER RANTZEN

LESS ENERGETIC
GAMES

THE PSYCHIATRIST'S GAME
or INSANE DELUSIONS

While one person is outside the room, the others decide upon a 'problem' that they all share: for example, that they all think they are the Queen, or that they only ever wear orange. The 'psychiatrist' returns, and has to guess the problem by asking each person a question. It can be any question whatsoever – what's your name, where do you live, how old are you – and the 'patients' must imagine themselves in their chosen role and answer accordingly. The psychiatrist can only ask one question at a time of each person and must then go on to the next person; and the question can, if he wishes, be a guess at diagnosing the problem. You can either give the psychiatrist a finite number of questions or let him go on asking questions until he gets the answer.

FRANCES EDMONDS

Variation:

I recollect playing this quite fascinating game at one party where there were about twenty people present. The interlocutor's quest was to establish not so much insane delusions as simple rules, such as 'Every answer given must start with a T', 'Each player must answer for the player on his left', 'Every third player must lie' and so on. After hours of amusement the players became so adept at the game that the outsider eventually guessed that 'The rule for this round is that there is no rule' within five minutes.

JOHN JUNKIN

CROSSED AND UNCROSSED

The object of the game is for the players to guess the object of the game. The leader informs the party guests that they are going to sit in a circle and pass around a pair of scissors. They can open or close the blades or leave them as they are, and each player will make the statement 'Crossed' or 'Uncrossed' before passing them on. However, this statement refers not to the scissors, but to whether the legs or ankles of the speaker are crossed or uncrossed. (For this reason the legs of the players must obviously be on view, so naturally the game can't be played while sitting around a table.)

The players then pass around the scissors, opening or closing them at will and stating 'Crossed' or 'Uncrossed'; the leader adding 'Correct' or 'Incorrect' depending on whether the player has made the correct observation. Obviously only those who have played the game before or have understood the secret will know what on earth is going on. Players may cross or uncross their legs at any time during the game, which lasts until everyone has guessed that the scissors are in fact merely a prop and that the statements refer to whether or not the speaker has his or her legs crossed.

DELIA SMITH

Variation:

In another game in which the object is to discover the object of the game, one person, whose name, say, is Jack, announces he is having a party, to which he is going to bring, say, some Jaffa cakes. The next person in the circle has to say what they will bring to the party – the key being that whatever they say they will bring must begin with the first letter of their own name. Thus Susan could bring satsumas to the party but not oranges. Everyone continues to take turns, the person giving the party accepting or rejecting what each person says they're bringing (and it doesn't matter how preposterous it is) until everyone has guessed the key.

LEUKAEMIA RESEARCH FUND

KIM'S GAME

Before the party, place about twenty disparate items on a tray and cover them with a cloth. When all your guests are present, bring in the tray and uncover it for a short time – half a minute's long enough. Cover the items again, remove the tray and give each guest a pencil and piece of paper. The guests then have to write down all the items they can remember, the winner being the one who can remember the greatest number of items.

SANDY LYLE

THIS IS MY LEFT EAR

This is an exceptionally silly game, even sillier than 'Poor Pussy' (see page 135). The assembled company sits in a circle.

The game is played clockwise. The first person touches, for example, his left ear and says 'This is my foot.' The next person must touch his/her foot (as

145

that is what the last person said) saying 'This is my right elbow.' The player after that touches his/her right elbow (as that is what the last person said) saying 'This is my nose.' In a short time someone will touch his/her chin and say 'This is my chin.' That person is then out because he/she told the truth.

IAN MESSITER

This is my left ear

EXHAUSTED TIGERS

A game that is a whiz for the very young and their exhausted carers at tea parties. They all lie on the floor and the first one to giggle or speak is out. You can put heads on tummies which increases the hilarity but shortens the peace and quiet.

LADY VICTORIA LEATHAM

ALIBI

Two guests leave the room and concoct an alibi within ten minutes as to their supposed actions within a twenty-four-hour period. The storyline can be as fanciful as they choose, just so long as the details of their alibis are correct.

The first guest then rejoins the other guests, who question him or her for a period of five minutes about the events of the twenty-four-hour period spent with the other guest. He/she then changes places with the partner outside the room – this prevents cheating by means of facial expressions or hand signals while the second player is questioned. The second guest is then closely questioned for five minutes by the other guests, who are naturally anxious to find flaws in his or her alibi. If the second guest fails to corroborate details of the events as related by his/her partner, both guests must pay a forfeit.

Another couple then leave the room and the game continues.

FIONA FULLERTON

THE CHRISTMAS CARD GAME

This game is particularly suitable for playing on Boxing Day evening.

All the Christmas cards received that year are placed face downwards on the floor and each player picks a hand, up to an agreed number of cards. The number should depend on the number of cards available and the number of players, and the more of both the better the game.

Some time before the game starts the organiser should have written on separate slips of paper a number of categories appropriate to the cards. For instance, prettiest snow scene, fattest robin, largest number of wings (including angelic wings), ugliest baby, the card with the most glitter, the most tasteless card, etc.

The players sit in a circle and in turn draw out one of these slips of paper from a hat. The category is read out and each player discards a Christmas card from their hand, if possible appropriate to that category. The players then have to decide corporately which card wins and if necessary to vote on it. The player who threw the winning card scores one point. The game proceeds with each player in turn drawing a category out of the hat and whoever scores the most points wins.

This is a gentle game but it can cause a lot of amusement, particularly when played with about a dozen people.

THE MOST REVD DR JOHN HABGOOD,
ARCHBISHOP OF YORK

FAMILY SNAP

No playing cards are required for this version of 'Snap'. A list of imaginary names is written on a sheet of paper, ensuring that there are about twice the number of names as actual players. The imaginary names should be very similar, the object being to cause confusion rather than avoid it.

Examples might include:

Donald O'Donnell
Dougal McDonald
Mr Douglas McDougall
Master Donald McDougall
Major Ronald O'Connell
and so on

A leader allocates an imaginary name to each guest, and calls out all the imaginary names at random every few seconds, ensuring that those names not allocated to players are of course included too. The players yell out 'Snap!" when they hear the name allocated to an actual participant, as opposed to an unallocated character. Points are won or lost as follows:

·   shouting 'Snap!' for the name allocated to another player – wins three points;
·   shouting 'Snap!' for the name allocated to yourself – wins one point;
·   shouting 'Snap!' for the name not allocated to another player – loses one point.

THE RT HON MICHAEL HOWARD MP

THE MOOSE AND THE KARIBU

This game is a riot whether you play it or watch it being played, for reasons that will follow.

Players sit in a circle and should be not fewer than

eight in number. In what follows the players will be assumed to be sitting in the positions of clock hours. The leader sits at the 12 o'clock position.

The leader hands to 1 o'clock an object, say an apple, and says 'This is a moose.' 1 o'clock replies, 'A what?' 12 o'clock replies, 'A moose.' 1 o'clock passes the object to 2 o'clock saying, 'This is a moose.' 2 o'clock hands it back saying 'A what?' and 1 o'clock shows it to 12 o'clock and says 'A what?' 12 o'clock says 'A moose,' and 1 o'clock returns it to 2 o'clock saying again 'This is a moose.' This ludicrous procedure goes on as each number passes the object to his next-door neighbour, ending with 11 o'clock handing the object back to 12 o'clock with the words 'This is a moose.'

This is a moose!

Meanwhile, the same procedure is going on in an anticlockwise direction with a different object and with the words 'This is a karibu,' and the karibu is similarly passed all the way round the clock until it reaches 12 o'clock again.

The trouble begins when the moose and the karibu are arriving at the same place (usually round about 6 o'clock) at the same time and the words 'A what?' from two directions. It is very unlikely that the player in the 6 o'clock position will keep his head and know in what direction the objects are passing, and is likely to forget the drill. All experience shows that the game usually breaks up in disorder at this point and that is really the best part of the game.

LEUKAEMIA RESEARCH FUND

DIVERSIONS

BLOW THE CANDLE OUT

A lighted candle is placed in the middle of the dinner table and each of the guests in turn is blindfolded, spun around three times and told to blow the candle out. It's much harder than it sounds, as guests stagger towards the doorway or window, puffing and blowing at thin air.

Variations:
When a player is blindfolded, you can blow the candle out yourself, so even if he or she advances in the right direction there'll still be a lot of huffing and puffing at nothing at all.

RUTH MADOC

ROUND THE ROOM

Did you play this in bored moments at school: see how far round a room you could get without touching the floor? From chair to table, to another chair, a leap on to the sofa, over the back and teeter round the rim of the fitted bookcase. Best for the young and light, and not very popular with the parents.

LEUKAEMIA RESEARCH FUND

THE CHAIR GAME

This game is really for chaps only (the fatter the funnier) but some women can do it.

Take three chairs – sturdy dining-room chairs are best, but not massive Victorian jobs or delicate Chippendale. Place one in the middle of the room (plenty of room is needed) on which a chap sits sideways. Another chair is then placed so his heels just rest on the edge of it; then, leaning back, his head is placed on a third. So he is lying across one chair, supported by just his heels and his head on the other two. The game is for him to pass the middle chair round his body; it calls for strong stomach muscles since all the support he gets is from his heels and head, and more often than not he descends in a heap on the floor. There's a slight danger that the middle chair might get a bit bashed as it completes the circle and has to be brought back under the somewhat sagging bottom, so it's best to use a kitchen chair for the middle one.

LEUKAEMIA RESEARCH FUND

THE MATCHBOX GAME

One matchbox cover (the box type, not book) is placed upright on the floor. The players take it in turn to put their clasped hands behind their backs and pick up the matchbox cover without touching the floor. You do it by going into a crouch and shoving one leg out sideways for balance and then leaning forward until you can pick up the matchbox in your teeth. It is simply a matter of balance, and the more athletic are quite able to do it. But most people lean forward slowly and then pitch forward on to their noses or shoulders, etc., the cause of much hilarity for the other players.

LEUKAEMIA RESEARCH FUND

SPOONING JELLY

Two players at a time are blindfolded and have to spoon-feed jelly to one another.

Variation:
Occasionally it's fun to leave the blindfold off one of

157

the players, but contrive it so his/her blindfolded partner doesn't know it.

LEUKAEMIA RESEARCH FUND

ROCKET GAME

A game for the young and the not-so-young alike.
Players stand in a small circle facing inwards.
First, all of them together make the noise of a match
being taken out of a matchbox, then the sound of the
match being struck. They all then pretend to apply
the lighted match to a rocket. All together they
exclaim, *fortissimo*, 'WHOOSH!' After a few seconds
everyone very quietly makes the absurd 'Pop' noise a
rocket makes in the air. All together they gasp 'What
a lovely rocket!'; then 'Mind the stick!' at which they
crouch down in terror, hands behind the head.
Absurd? Yes! But ludicrous fun.

LEUKAEMIA RESEARCH FUND

PERFORMING AN OPERATION

Shine a light on a sheet in a dark room. Behind the
sheet a couple take the parts of the 'doctor' and
'patient' and their silhouettes are watched by the other
guests on the other side of the sheet. The various stages
of an operation are mimed, with such things as sausages

and spaghetti being used as the organs. These are put into a bowl and passed around in the dark.

LEUKAEMIA RESEARCH FUND

THE BROOM GAME

For this game you need a broom (garden or otherwise) and plenty of open space. It is very dangerous to attempt it in a confined space or near hard items such as garden walls, etc.

The victim stands in the middle of the lawn, with arms fully extended upwards, and the broom head held above the head. Looking at the broom in that position, the victim must circle ten times, keeping the broom both aloft and at the centre of the circle, i.e. as the pivot around which the manoeuvre is made.

On completion of the circling, the victim must immediately bring the broom down so that the head of the broom rests on the ground, and attempt to step on the broom head. It is by no means easy to do so while remaining upright, hence the need for much space.

DAVID GOWER

WHICH BOOK?

Take any nine books (in their jackets so the titles are clear) and lay them out quite close together in three rows of three. Two people perform the trick, which is supposed to be a matter of telepathy between the two. The assistant/stooge goes out of the room and the MC asks the assembled company to choose a book which is the one that the stooge is to guess correctly when he comes back into the room. Let us assume the party guests decide that the third book in the top row (i.e. the one in the top right-hand corner) is the book to be chosen, and it is to be chosen as the fourth book marked.

Back into the room comes the stooge. The MC makes all the usual noises about is your head clear, are you concentrating, look into my eyes, etc. Then the MC – with the aid of a walking stick – taps one of the books (not the one) and asks: 'Is it this one?' That first point is the vital clue to the stooge because where the stick is placed tells him/her which book the party has chosen. This is done by dividing the first book pointed at into nine imaginary squares – 3 x 3 books – and the tip of the walking stick has to be lightly placed (just a dab: long enough for the stooge to check the position but not lingered upon) in the top right-hand corner of that first book. This tells the stooge that the chosen book is in the top right-hand corner of the books on the floor. 'Not that one,' the stooge will reply. The MC then points to another two books, placing the stick in any position on them so to the eyes of the party, he is just pointing out the books in turn. 'No, no,' will say the stooge. Then the MC will point – in any position – to the selected book (as requested by the party, it is the fourth book to be pointed out) and the stooge will say 'Yessir, that's the one.'

It's very simple really, and actually it does intrigue people.

LEUKAEMIA RESEARCH FUND

MEET LORD NELSON

One person is blindfolded, led around the room and introduced to lots of people or things supposedly related to Lord Nelson, such as Lady Hamilton, Hardy, a cannonball from the *Victory*, Nelson's sword, etc. The leader finally introduces the person to Lord Nelson himself, then says, 'And this is Lord Nelson's eye,' pushing the victim's finger into a peeled grape or lychee.

LEUKAEMIA RESEARCH FUND

ATHLETE AND SPOON

I first came across this game in 1982 when I was staying at the Gold Coast, near Brisbane, Australia, with a number of my fellow athletes preparing for the Commonwealth Games. A large, male thrower was persuaded to sit on a chair with his head down and another athlete placed a table spoon in his mouth. It was stated that by manoeuvring his head, the second athlete would strike the seated athlete's head with the spoon. What actually happened was that a third athlete nipped in behind the seated athlete, who could not see him because his head was down, and struck him on the head with another spoon.

The game continued with a different athlete sitting on the chair with his head down and another athlete attempting to strike him on the head with a spoon held in his mouth. This was watched by the first victim. On this occasion, there was no third person to nip in and administer a blow.

The first victim returned to the chair on at least eight occasions before the game was finished and, to this day, the very large athlete (who could have thrown us all out of the window of the seventh-floor flat where he was staying!) does not know the true story, still believing that the person with the spoon in his mouth was very skilful to have given him such a decisive blow on the head.

FATIMA WHITBREAD

GROWN-UP GAMES

THE VICIOUS DREAM GAME or SMILE AND SMILE AND BE A VILLAIN

This is a monstrous game and the one or two people who I have played it on have never properly recovered. The game is central to the old English tradition of house-party nastiness in which characters are destroyed and egos disassembled with a winning smile. The game, whose purpose is humiliation, is only to be wheeled out in a spirit of pure loathing.

Tell your bitterest enemy to leave the room and wait while the rest of you think up the sort of dream he might have. The dream is quite detailed, with specific incidents and characters. Then he must return, ask questions which have yes or no answers and try to discover what the dream is.

The enemy leaves the room and you let the others into the secret. We do not think up a dream at all. Instead, we agree that if a question ends in a vowel we shall answer yes and if with a consonant no. One ending with the letter 'y' is to be answered, 'Maybe, probably'.

This takes ten seconds to explain but the enemy has to imagine we are dreaming up something utterly revealing about his character and so we all have another glass of whisky for ten minutes while his imagination festers outside.

He is summoned back, anxious and depressed because he has heard the echoes of unkind laughter coming from the sitting room.

'It's bound to be about that thing at school with Pilkington.'

'No,' we say.

'Oh, God, not Hobhouse?'

'Yes.'

'When I bullied him?'

'No.'

'You mean he's bullying me?'

'Yes.'

'But how on earth did you know I ever bullied him?'

'We didn't, we just dreamt it up.'

'Is he doing it with the treacle?'

'Yes.'

'And I'm screaming for help?'

'No.'

'You mean I'm quite enjoying it, really?'

'Well, sort of.'

'Am I kneeling at his feet?'

'No.'

'Or are we lying head to toe?' Nicholas asks with the horror of true recognition.

'Yes, Nicholas, you are lying head to toe, with Hobhouse, and the treacle, and you are at least sort of enjoying it.'

Whether this can really be called a family game, I don't know. It can go on for as long as your cruelty lasts, travelling deep into the recesses of Nicholas's own fantasies and memories. He is left sobered and ashamed. It's a perfectly horrible game.

ADAM NICOLSON

FIRST NIGHT OF THE HONEYMOON

A couple leave the room, and the remaining guests are told to listen to their comments on their return as if they were made on the first night of the honeymoon.

The couple are invited back into the room and told to perform an innocuous task in front of the others, though naturally no mention is made of the fact that the other guests are going to regard their comments in a somewhat different light.

A popular task set is to tell the couple to get inside one massive mackintosh at the same time, or to put (some of) one another's clothes on back to front, to walk a short distance atop a wine bottle, or to attempt to remove three items of each other's clothing while blindfolded. In each case their advice and comments to each other while performing the allotted tasks provide much amusement for the other guests.

NED SHERRIN

A GROWN-UP GAME

This is a game for the grown-up members of the family. It is best played in twos; I used to play it with my cousin. Each goes into a room and takes his place at a table with a glass and a bottle of Scotch whisky. Each drinks his bottle. Then one goes out, knocks on the door and the other has to guess who it is.

DEREK NIMMO

RUDE SCRABBLE ®

This game is for adults only and involves the use of a Scrabble ® board and letters. You can't play it when you're at home; it's designed for playing in airport lounges and public rooms in hotels where strangers may wander by, look at the board and read what you've done. You get double scores for dirty words and triple scores for the most appalling words you can think of. If you've got the nerve to put them down, is the argument, you're entitled to the extra number on your score board!

CLAIRE RAYNER

MEXICANO

This is a drinking game that as many or as few people as you like can play. Two dice. The first person who throws the dice has up to three attempts to throw the highest score possible. Two sixes is obviously the highest throw (and entitles that player to an extra free throw). The object of the game is to try to get a 'mexicano' throw which is a two and a one. The forfeit attached to this means that the person with the lowest score drinks a double measure. There can be an unlimited number of 'mexicano' throws per round.

There is a throw called 'snake eyes' which is a throw of two ones. In this case the round is automatically stopped and that player drinks the forfeit in the middle of the table. There is a throw of a four and a three which means that player has to ask everyone a trivia question that has to be deemed reasonable. If the others answer the question correctly the questioner drinks, but if they cannot answer the question everyone round the table drinks.

When the first person has thrown, for instance, a five and a four on their second throw, this means that everyone else has only two chances to get a higher score. If at the end of the round (i.e. when everyone has thrown the dice) two people have thrown the same lowest score, there is a spin-off and the lowest scorer of that device is the one who drinks.

All very silly really but can be hugely enjoyable!

LEUKAEMIA RESEARCH FUND

SURGEON'S KNOCK

A boy and girl go outside and stay there till she says 'Cut it out!'
Sorry.

JOHN JUNKIN

INDEX

INDEX OF GAMES

Add Your Own Line to a
  Famous Poem's First 26
Adverbs (or In the Manner of
  the Word) 58
Advertising 34
Alibi 147
All Change 121
The Alphabet Game see Boy
  Girl Boy Girl
Animal Game, The 97
Animal Snap 109
Are You There, Moriarty? 127
Arms and Legs 49
Athlete and Spoon 161

Backwards and Forwards 133
Balderdash 30
Ball and Spoon Race 134
The Balloon Game 131
Balloon Treasure Hunt 46
Battleships 39
A Beach Game 48
Beating the Plate 128
The Bellman 47
Biblical Treasure Hunt 47
Blind Man's Dip (or The
  Game) 36
Blow the Candle Out 155
Blowing up the Balloon and
  Bursting It 131
Botticelli 74
Bottle Walking 133
Boy Girl Boy Girl (or The
  Alphabet Game or
  Categories) 37
The Broom Game 159

Caboosh 111
The Car Numbers Game 51
Categories see Boy Girl Boy
  Girl
Category One Two 98
The Chair Game 156
Charades 57
Cheat 109
Chinese Whispers 102
Chocolate Game 119
The Christmas Card Game
  147

Clapping Games 96
Coin Game 130
Consequences 23
Cricket on the Move 50
Crambo 79
Crossed and Uncrossed 144

Dead Horses 18
Dentist's Despair see The
  Sweet Game
Description Switch 89
A Dice Game 101
The Dictionary Game 29
The Dictionary Game with
  Books 32
Dog Spotting 50
The Drawing Game (or
  Pictionary) 38

European Game 28
Exhausted Tigers 146

The Family Coach 123
Family Snap 148
Fanning the Kipper 132
First Night of the
  Honeymoon 167
Fizz-Buzz 96
Flour Cake Game 120
Frances Hodgson Burnett's
  Game 90

The Game 60
The Game see Blind Man's Dip
Ghost 87
Gritty Uvula 88
A Grown-up Game 167
Guess the Feet 137
Guess the Profession 48

The Hat Game 71
Headlines 35
How, When, Where and
  Why? 86
Hunt the Kipper 121

I Love My Love 83
I Went to Paris 65
If You Were … 73
In the Manner of the Word *see*
    Adverbs
Insane Delusions *see* The
    Psychiatrist's Game

Kick-the-Can 45
Kim's Game 145

Limerick Game 25
Literary Styles 28
Long Botticelli 75

Make Your Noise, Animal 122
The Matchbox Game 157
Meet Lord Nelson 161
Mexicano 168
Monosyllables 78
The Moose and the Karibu 149
Mummies and Daddies 123
Murder by Winking 100

Nell Gwynne's Game 119
Newspapers on a Train 125
Number Plates 51
Numerical Phrases 80

The Obstacle Course 130
Old Maid 110

Pairs 108
Pea Picking 135
Performing an Operation 158
Pictionary *see* The Drawing
    Game
Ping-Pong Table Football 99
Poet's Chair 81
The Poetry Game 24
Poor Pussy 135
Prime Rhymes (*or* Stinky
    Pinky) 85
Proverbs 76
The Psychiatrist's Game (*or*
    Insane Delusions) 143

The Quotation Game 31
The Railway Carriage
    Game 76
The Return of the Emperor 63
Rhyming Dumbshow 59
Rocket Game 158
Round the Room 156
Rude Scrabble ® 168

Scissors, Paper and Stone 101
Scrub a Fairy 27
Shop Snap 108
Silent Chinese Whispers 59
Smile and Smile and Be a
    Villain *see* The Vicious
    Dream Game
Soap-savers Game 126
Spooning Jelly 157
Spoons 107
A Stay-awake Game 53
Stinky Pinky *see* Prime Rhymes
Super-Ghost 87
Surgeon's Knock 169
The Sweet Game (*or* Dentist's
    Despair) 138

Taboo 78
The Tennis-Elbow-Foot
    Game 80
This Is My Left Ear 145
Torch Solitaire 17
Twenty Questions (*or* Who
    Am I?) 70

Up Jenkins 95

The Vicious Dream Game (*or*
    Smile and Smile and Be a
    Villain) 165
Video Fun 136

Wanderer's Game 83
What Am I? 69
Which Book? 159
Who Am I? *see* Twenty
    Questions
Wrong Name Game 77

INDEX OF CONTRIBUTORS

John Alderton 18
The Marquess of Anglesey 25
Pamela Armstrong 85
Jane Asher 60
Michael Aspel 80

Beryl Bainbridge 64
Jeremy Beadle 63
Lynda Bellingham 103
Honor Blackman 80
Rabbi Lionel Blue 47
Ian and Kathy Botham 30
The Rt Hon Virginia
  Bottomley MP 29
The Earl of Bradford 23
Gyles Brandreth MP 76, 91
Richard Branson 77
Michael Buerk 58

Cheryl Campbell 34
Willie Carson 65
Sebastian Coe MP 122
Pauline Collins 191
Rosemary Conley 38
Sue Cook 86
Colin Cowdrey 108
Wendy Craig 47
Leslie Crowther 49
Edwina Currie MP 119

Paul Daniels 102
Dame Judi Dench 89
David Dimbleby 125

Frances Edmonds 143

Nick and Gill Faldo 49
Rachel Heyhoe Flint 50
Fiona Fullerton 147

Mike Gatting 99
Rumer Godden 30
David Gower 159
Lucinda Green 46
Sarah Greene 71

The Most Revd Dr John
  Habgood, Archbishop of
  York 148
The Rt Revd Richard Harries,
  Bishop of Oxford 96
Damon Hill 35
Min Hogg 77, 89
Gordon Honeycombe 41
The Rt Hon Michael Howard
  MP 149
Gareth Hunt 110
James Hunt 87

Tony Jacklin 69
David Jacobs 100
Stratford Johns 133
John Junkin 143, 169

Felicity Kendal 107
HRH the Duke of Kent 57

The Rt Hon Norman Lamont
  MP 35
Nigella Lawson 73
Lady Victoria Leatham 146
Virginia Leng 133
Leukaemia Research Fund 26,
  26, 98, 109, 116, 120,
  120,123, 123, 126, 129,
  131, 132, 145, 151, 156,
  156, 157, 158, 158, 159,
  160, 161, 169
Maureen Lipman 109
Sam Llewellyn 31, 53, 75
The Countess of Longford 58
Sandy Lyle 145

Sir Ian McKellen 31
Ruth Madoc 155
Alfred Marks 136
Christopher Martin-Jenkins
  28, 32
Ian Messiter 69, 79, 83, 88,
  135, 137, 146
Jean Metcalfe 51, 81
Cliff Michelmore 51, 81

Guy Michelmore 135
Dr Patrick Moore 96
Sir Jeremy Morse 33
Nicholas Mosley 25
Stirling Moss 134
Jimmy Mulville 38

Nanette Newman 73
Emma Nicholson MP 37
Adam Nicolson 166
Derek Nimmo 167

Lord Oaksey 39

Michael Parkinson 131
John Parrott 138
Jeremy Paxman 87
Julian Pettifer 101

Esther Rantzen 139
Claire Rayner 48, 52, 168
Anneka Rice 97
Natasha Richardson 34
Diana Rigg 32
Robert Robinson 50
Anton Rodgers 121
The Rt Hon Dame Angela
    Rumbold MP 130

Brough Scott 128
Fred Secombe 71
Jane Seymour 71
Ned Sherrin 167
Delia Smith 144
The Rt Hon Sir David   Steel
    MP 83
Imogen Stubbs 45
Janet Suzman 62

Rosie Thomas 28
Sandi Toksvig 34
John Tovey 48

Rory Underwood 111

Fatima Whitbread 162
Katharine Whitehorn 127
Simon Williams 39
Bob Wilson 100
The Rt Hon the Lord Wilson
    of Rievaulx 78
Helen Atkinson Wood 34

The Earl of Yarmouth 78

Michael York 59